Wine Wherever™

In California's Mid-Coast & Inland Regions

Wine Tasting in Monterey, Santa Clara and Santa Cruz Counties

by Dahlynn McKowen and Ken McKowen

Cheers!
Dahlynn McKowen

Ken McKowen

PS

Publishing Syndicate
Orangevale, California

PS

Wine Wherever: In California's Mid-Coast and Inland Regions
Wine Tasting in Monterey, Santa Clara and Santa Cruz Counties

First Edition 2011

Copyright 2011 by Dahlynn McKowen and Ken McKowen

Photos by the authors, except where noted
Maps: Lohnes+Wright GIS and Mapping
Cover and Book Design: Publishing Syndicate
Cover photo: Ridge Vineyards, Cupertino
Book Editor: Terri Elders

ISBN 978-0-9824654-5-5

Library of Congress Control Number 2011924595

Printed in Canada

Published by: **Publishing Syndicate**
PO Box 607
Orangevale, CA 95662
Fax 916-987-6501
Ken@PublishingSyndicate.com
www.PublishingSyndicate.com

Join our Facebook page: www.Facebook.com/WineWherever
Visit our website to see what other great books we offer!

NOTICE: Although Publishing Syndicate and the authors have made every attempt to ensure that the information in this book is accurate at press time, they are not responsible for any loss, damage, injury or inconvenience that may occur to anyone while using this book. You are responsible for your own safety and health while traveling. Always check local conditions, know your limitations and your vehicle's limitations, and, of course, don't drink and drive.

PLEASE USE A DESIGNATED DRIVER WHEN WINE TASTING!

To those wine lovers
who see their glasses
always half full,
never half empty.

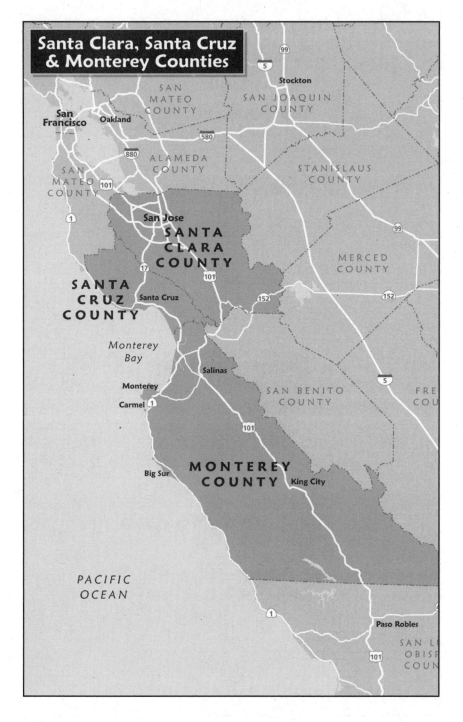

Contents

Chapter Three: Santa Cruz County   156

Welcome to Wine Country

This first in a series of *Wine Wherever* books focuses on California's Mid-Coast counties of Monterey and Santa Cruz and the adjacent inland county of Santa Clara. As national award-winning travel book authors, each of us possesses an avid interest in history and in people. Accordingly, the research we undertook and the resulting focus of our writing in *Wine Wherever* is meant to entertain and educate. We believe we amply illustrate that there is so much more to wine tasting than attempting to sample ten wines at a dozen wineries in a single day. Wine tasting is a wonderful adventure, not only for one's palate, but for the mind and body as well. Wine tasting provides opportunities to spend time relaxing with family and friends and enjoying the diverse ambiances created by the wineries. It's also an opportunity to meet people in the wine industry and explore their philosophies and approaches to winemaking.

During our research for this book, we visited every winery we wrote about and often got to know the owners, and sometimes their kids, pets, staff and the winemakers (when the winemaker wasn't the owner). The wineries we feature in our *Wine Wherever* books are those we would want to take our friends and family to visit—and we have—and not simply for their great wines, but also for each winery's history, entertainment opportunities, special events and friendly atmosphere. We spent countless hours talking with these folks. We would pose a simple question and more times than not we would hear wonderful explanations and funny stories from our new friends. We learned that no one could explain his or her wine in better detail and with as much passion as a devoted artisan winemaker. Portions of those stories are in this book and more detailed interviews, which we have noted in the story, can be found online at **www.WineWherever.com**. And for the record, there was no charge for the wineries to be in the book, and we didn't accept bribes to write only good things about them, although several owners insisted we take home bottles of their wine to enjoy later!

Wine in California

California's wine history began with the Spanish in 1769, when Father Junipero Serra founded his first mission in San Diego. Among his fields of grains, fruits and beans, he planted grapes to produce wine for religious purposes. It's likely that the Spanish soldiers in this lonely outpost also found uses for the Padre's wine. Missions and their related horticultural practices, including winemaking, spread northward from San Diego into Monterey in 1770, Santa Clara in 1777 and to Santa Cruz in 1791. While other varietal grapes were

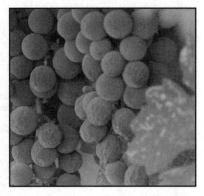

being introduced beginning about 1833, Father Serra's initial vines became known as the "Mission grape," and it dominated California's infant wine industry until the 1880s.

Accompanying California's thirsty Gold Rush 49ers, Hungarian immigrant Agoston Haraszthy began importing cuttings from dozens of different European grape varieties. In 1857, he founded California's first commercial winery in Sonoma and named it "Buena Vista Winery" (now Buena Vista Carneros). His varietal grapes soon found their way to many parts of California.

While California's wine industry flourished during the mid- to late-19th century, Europe's winemakers were taking a beating as a destructive root louse known as phylloxera was decimating their continent's vineyards. Phylloxera was a native grapevine pest in the United States and because collecting exotic plants was popular in the 1850s throughout Victorian Europe, botanists had imported American native grapevines, ignorant of phylloxera. The bug quickly spread, destroying much of Europe's wine production, especially the French wine industry. Finally, scientists discovered that native U.S. grapevines often survived because they had developed a reasonable immunity to the pest, so they began to graft European vine cuttings onto California grape rootstock. While Europe's vineyards struggled to revive themselves, California's wine industry thrived.

Even though phylloxera couldn't destroy California's wine industry, the U.S. government could, and did, for decades. The Volstead National Prohibition Act in 1919, and its related Eighteenth Amendment to the Constitution in 1920, prohibited the manufacture, sale and transport of intoxicating liquors, which included wine. With the market for fine wines wiped out, growers replaced their wine grape vineyards with fruit orchards or inexpensive, low-quality juice grapes. By 1925, wine production in California had dropped by 94 percent.

Only a few of the original varietal vines remained where government permits allowed for the limited production of wine for medicinal and religious purposes. Prohibition was repealed in 1933, and California flooded markets with cheap, poor-quality wine. Fortified dessert wines became very popular and outsold table wines until the 1960s. Prior to Prohibition there were 2,500 commercial wineries in the U.S. and 781 bonded wineries in California. When Prohibition ended, only 100 wineries remained in the entire nation and it would take 50 years before California once again reached 781 bonded wineries. Today, California's 3,000 federally-bonded wineries account for 90 percent of the wine produced in the U.S. If California were a country, it would be the fourth-largest producer of wine in the world.

The Central Coast Appellation

California is divided into five large wine regions or appellations: North Coast, Central Coast, South Coast, Central Valley and the Sierra Foothills. Within each of those appellations, numerous American Viticultural Areas (AVAs) exist. Often lots of little AVAs exist inside the larger AVAs, making their regional identification even more confusing. For example, the Central Coast AVA includes the Santa Cruz Mountains AVA, which contains the Ben Lomond Mountain AVA. For most people, AVAs or appellations mean little unless you're someone who has decided that only grapes from a specific region or AVA are adequate for your palate. One of the key features of an area being designated as an AVA is that its wineries can advertise on their labels that they belong to a par-

ticular AVA (i.e., a Santa Cruz Mountains wine or a Napa Valley wine). In order to qualify, 85 percent of the grapes used in that wine must come from the identified AVA.

For purposes of this book, we decided to mix things up a bit and go with a non-traditional regional subtitle: "Mid-Coast and Inland Regions." The term "mid-coast" represents the coastal region of the Golden State that stretches north to south, from the upper reaches of Santa Cruz County to Monterey's county line where it meets San Luis Obispo County. The term "inland region" represents the eastern side of the Santa Cruz Mountains and the Santa Clara Valley. While some may question our creative terminology for the title of this *Wine Wherever* book, we feel it is a fair descriptor of this unique and very dynamic wine area of California.

Wine Varietals and Blends

In the U.S., wines identified by the names on their labels as being a varietal—a single grape name such as Pinot Noir, Cabernet Sauvignon, Merlot, Zinfandel and so forth—must contain at least 75 percent of the named grape. In addition to varietals, many winemakers create excellent blends by mixing two or more varietal grapes, none of which reaches that magic 75-percent content requirement to be considered a single varietal. These blended wines end up with non-varietal names on their bottles such as "Crestview Gold" or "Karen's Creation" or "Artful Zinful."

Ignoring for a moment the official Central Coast AVA (that also includes Santa Barbara, San Luis Obispo and Contra Costa counties), during the past dozen years or so, Monterey, Santa Clara and Santa Cruz counties significantly have expanded their vineyards and increased the number of wineries, and additionally have matured as producers of fine wines. With climate differences that can range from inland hot to coastal cool, they are capable of producing wines similar to those grown in Bordeaux, France, including Cabernet Sauvignon, Cabernet Franc and Merlot, as well as Rhone varietals such as Syrah and Viognier. There also are Pinot Noir, associated with France's Burgundy region; Sangiovese, an Italian grape; the Spanish favorite Tempranillo; and even Riesling, a German Rhine region varietal. Monterey, Santa Clara and Santa Cruz counties also grow the popular varietals, Chardonnay and Zinfandel.

Many wineries, especially the smaller boutiques, specialize in a handful of varietals and perhaps a blend or two. Some wineries grow their own grapes, while many depend on grapes purchased from local or regional grape growers who are not necessarily winemakers. A few wineries also use grapes from outside their appellation.

Using This Book

Wine Wherever books are designed to be easy to use, comprehensive and fun. The series introduces wine lovers to stories about those unique and eclectic wineries and their just-as-interesting owners, winemakers and grape growers. This book, covering Monterey, Santa

Clara and Santa Cruz counties, is divided into three chapters, one for each county. Each chapter begins with an introduction that provides a short history of the county, much of it tied to the missions and early agriculture. We have included locator maps that correspond with each chapter's wineries. From there, you're free to peruse the many winery listings, discovering the richness of each destination and its contribution to the wine industry. And if you want to learn more about any particular winery, each listing has contact information, including a website. The "More Area Wineries" sections after the main listings in each chapter provide information on additional wineries not covered in detail.

Historic Monterey Custom House

There is much to see and do throughout California's Mid-Coast and Inland regions in addition to visiting the wineries. No wine-tasting trip would be complete without enjoying some of the hundreds of other attractions found here: historic old towns, lighthouses, missions, state parks and the spectacular coast itself with its beaches. We include suggested side trips with enough information to whet your appetite for a little adventure. We also provide at the close of each chapter a contact list for local and regional visitor bureaus, wine organizations and other relevant resources.

Selection Criteria

While using this book, you'll find that wineries weren't selected simply based on size or how many gold medals their wines have won. The wineries featured herein range from mom-and-pop operations that deliver as little as a hundred cases a year to those household names that produce 500,000 cases a year. Some wineries have won dozens of gold medals over the years; others with equally excellent wines choose not to enter such competitions, instead letting customers decide how good their wines are.

Those wineries featured by way of a full story qualified for such because: 1) They completed our required consideration survey, providing enough information to help us create a usable story, 2) They regularly post public hours and maintain an active website, and 3) When we visited each candidate winery, we determined their business was worthy of being included. Other listed wineries include those who responded but did not complete the survey in full or with enough detail to warrant a full story, or those who are reputable wineries in that particular region that warrant inclusion. If we have inadvertently missed a winery or two, we offer apologies in advance. But we did our best, considering that we contacted more than 170 wineries and visited more than 100 of them while doing our research. And we indeed thank all of our friends who offered to go along with us as "research buddies"—if we had actually tasted all the wines graciously offered at each winery, this book would still be in its first draft!

While we're on the topic of tasting, the reason we don't "partake" at most of the wineries is that we are not—in any way, shape or form—wine critics. We're simply wine lovers. It wouldn't be fair for us to formally evaluate any winery's bottled offerings because, quite honestly, almost all offer great wines and choosing the "best" wine from among the hundreds of tastings offered  would be subjective. While some may consider the stereotypical "Two-Buck Chuck" (Charles Shaw) to be a good wine buy, others prefer more complex wines that typically cost more than $2 a bottle. For this reason, we usually don't go much beyond mentioning those varietals that a winery is most proud of and known for and leave it at that. As the old saying goes, "To each his own." Everyone's taste buds are different, which means nobody is ever 100-percent right about what constitutes a great wine, a good wine or even a bad wine. How do you choose a great bottle of wine from among the thousands of choices out there? It's easy—sample the wines and then buy what you like.

With this book in hand, it's time for you to head to this wonderful wine region. Taste, experience and enjoy—and take a few bottles home to share with family and friends. They will love you for it.

Before You Go

Before you go, be sure to contact the winery or check the destination's website as hours of operation can change without notice and often change between winter and summer. Their contact information appears at the end of each listing. Or complement this book by downloading a free *Wine Wherever Mid-Coast* mobile app (see the last section of this intro for more info).

Also, if you will be visiting via a tour bus or limousine service, we strongly encourage you to notify the wineries you wish to visit *prior* to your arrival. While many will welcome you with open arms, others require advance notification or they will not serve you and your party, or they may charge an additional tasting fee.

As true wine lovers know—and winemakers and winery owners will concede—operating a winery is a business, and that business needs sales to keep offering inexpensive or complimentary tastings. Quite simply, if you love a wine, please buy a bottle or two or an entire case, and show your support for these wonderful wineries.

If you use GPS, be aware that the required guidance satellites aren't always reachable through the tall trees and steep mountains. Old fashioned maps may serve you better.

Website Bonus

During our travels through Monterey, Santa Cruz and Santa Clara counties, we learned so much that we couldn't fit it all into this book. On our website (**www.WineWherever.com**), you'll find in-depth interviews with numerous winemakers and winery owners from this region. These people are passionate about their craft and their wines; you'll learn what makes them tick and why they love the business. Plus, you'll enjoy their unique senses of humor. And boy, do they have some intriguing stories to share. We're always adding more interviews—so visit often.

We can't forget the food! People always ask about which wines to pair with which foods. Winemakers will tell you to drink the wines you love with the foods you like to eat. There are no set rules for what wines go with which foods. Pairing your favorite port with rich, chocolate brownies will likely add to the pleasure of both, as might combining crab cakes with a Chardonnay, Viognier or Merlot. Several wineries offer pairing opportunities, especially at their wine club member dinners. If you would like to investigate dozens of great food and wine pairing suggestions and recipes, go to **www.WineWherever.com.** We are constantly adding new food and wine pairing ideas, along with delicious recipes shared with us by some of our favorite winemakers and winery owners.

Besides the interviews and food, our website includes fun photographs, a link to our *Wine Wherever* **Facebook** page (www.Facebook. com/WineWherever) and links to all of the winery websites included in our books. You can also sign-up for our quarterly e-newsletter that includes winery updates, feature articles and winery discount coupons, plus announcements regarding new *Wine Wherever* books and apps.

Wine Wherever Mobile Apps

Which winery should we try next?" is an oft-asked question posed by wine tasters. We created the *Wine Wherever* mobile apps to quickly answer that question! With location-aware mapping capabilities, coupled with a list of nearly every winery open on a regular schedule for public wine tasting, you instantly will learn the location of the next closest winery. *Wine Wherever* apps feature wine journaling capabilities, where you can log your tastes right into your device: taste now, remember later! The apps also sport telephone and website contacts with just a tap of a button. And, they include special money-saving coupons for nearby wineries, restaurants, B&Bs and more.

Wine Wherever apps, which are free, also include a list of conversation-starter questions you might ask at tasting rooms. And for those new to wine tasting, we have included a section that provides proper wine-tasting etiquette, such as not wearing heavy perfume or cologne. The odor will overwhelm the flavor nuances of any wine—both for you and for everyone around you.

As of this writing, we have developed *Wine Wherever* apps for nine California wine regions—Central Valley, Mid-Coast, Napa, North Coast, Paso Robles, Santa Barbara, Sierra Foothills, Sonoma and South Coast—along with apps for the states of New York, Oregon, Texas and Washington. Download the free app via your app store or for more information visit **www.WineWherever.com.**

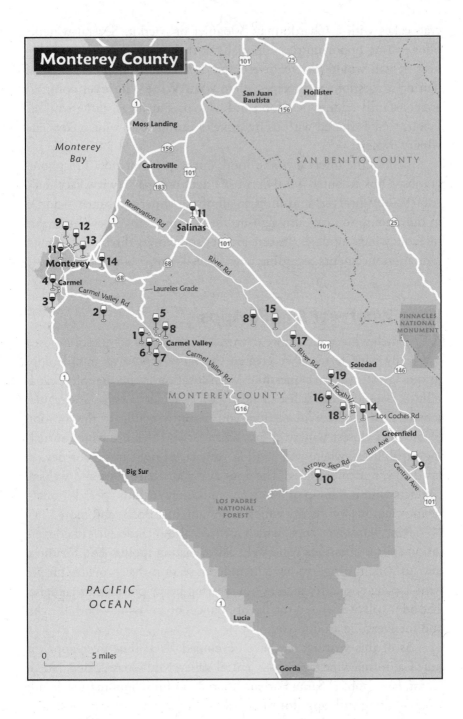

Monterey County

101
25

San Juan
Bautista
Hollister

156

Moss Landing

*Monterey
Bay*

156

Castroville

SAN BENITO COUNTY

101

183

Reservation Rd

9 12
13
11
Monterey

1

11
Salinas

101

25

River Rd

14

68

68

— Laureles Grade

4 Carmel

3

Carmel Valley Rd

2

5

8

15

8

PINNACLES
NATIONAL
MONUMENT

1

1

Carmel Valley

17

6 7

River Rd

101

Carmel Valley Rd

Soledad

146

MONTEREY COUNTY

19

16

Foothill Rd

14

G16

18

Los Coches Rd

Greenfield

Big Sur

Elm Ave

Arroyo Seco Rd

9

Central Ave

10

101

LOS PADRES
NATIONAL
FOREST

*PACIFIC
OCEAN*

1

Lucia

0   5 miles

Gorda

Chapter One

Monterey County is, without a doubt, home to one of the nation's most fertile farmlands. Farming has been a part of the county's rich history since the late 1700s when the Spanish established their missions in Carmel, Soledad and San Antonio. It was then that Mission wine grapes were planted, an important fruit that the Franciscan friars used to make their sacramental wine. Other crops were planted, including wheat and corn, which helped support the missionaries and neophytes who lived and worked at the missions.

While farming continued to thrive in Monterey County, it wasn't until the 1960s that wine grapes were reintroduced to the fertile region. Professor A.J. Winkler, a viticultural authority from the University of California at Davis, published a report comparing the Monterey County region favorably with the premium wine regions of Napa, Sonoma, Burgundy and Bordeaux. The professor's report proved ac-

curate. Monterey's coastal mountains, inland valleys, great soils and the coastal-tempered climate had made Monterey County one of California's premier wine producers. Soon after the report was released, large corporations began acquiring Monterey County land for the huge vineyards needed to supply their anticipated demand for premium "fruit wine" and "dessert wine" offerings. From just five acres of vines in 1966 to 2,000 acres in 1970 to more than 40,000 acres today, there appears to be no end to the expansion of vineyards throughout this region.

Within the boundaries of the broad Monterey AVA (American Viticultural Area), which is part of the Central Coast AVA, lie several smaller AVAs including Carmel Valley, Arroyo Seco and Santa Lucia Highlands. Each AVA claims its own special microclimates and soils, creating different, yet exceptional, grape-growing characteristics. Within Monterey's wine region you will enjoy some of California's biggest producing wineries, along with small boutique wineries. And it's not uncommon at many of the smaller wineries for the owners or winemakers to pour for you.

If you don't have a designated driver or would prefer not to taste and drive, hop aboard the Carmel Valley Grapevine Express. The Grapevine Express is the name of the local transit agency's convenient bus service for spring and summer visitors. Buses leave from downtown Monterey every hour and stop at many wineries enroute to Carmel Valley Village; in Carmel Valley, numerous tasting rooms are bunched within easy walking distance of one another (Monterey-Salinas Transit: www.mst.org).

One oddity we must point out is that downtown Carmel is actually the incorporated city of Carmel-by-the-Sea. For purposes of the book, this city is listed as such in the alphabetical winery listings. Even odder is that addresses in Carmel-by-the-Sea lack physical numerical street references. For example, the address under Galante Vineyard's listing is "Dolores Avenue between Ocean and 7th." Your best bet is to pick up a map from any business in this area—all are happy and eager to help tourists navigate their way around the city.

After a day of wine tasting, there is plenty more to see and do in Monterey County. The City of Monterey's historic downtown features adobe homes and other buildings remaining from California's Spanish and Mexican eras. Many, including the restored Custom House, adjacent to the always-popular Fisherman's Wharf, are open to the public as part of Monterey State Historic Park. Beautiful Point Lobos State Reserve, the northern gateway to the spectacular Big Sur Coast, is located just a few miles south of Carmel. There's also the National Steinbeck Center, an excellent museum in Salinas dedicated to author John Steinbeck. And, Monterey's famed Cannery Row, where Steinbeck once frequented, offers numerous fine restaurants, gift shops, several winery tasting rooms and the world-class Monterey Bay Aquarium.

Monterey's Fisherman's Wharf

Carmel

1 Boëté Winery

For grape growers and winemakers John and Jana Saunders, the first step in making exceptional wines was to find the perfect piece of land. In 1994 the couple purchased 14 acres in the Carmel Valley. Three years later they planted what they knew in their hearts would become a vineyard worthy of producing world-class wines. Saunders' vineyard did just that, with its south-facing slopes and Bordeaux clones soaking in all the wonderful sunshine and nutrients from the fine terroir the Carmel Valley has to offer.

The Saunders sold grapes to other wineries for several years, opening Boëté Winery (pronounced bwah-TAY) in 2000. The winery is named after John's maternal grandparents—François and Jeannie Boëté—who immigrated to the United States in the 1930s from the little town of Le Juch in the Brittany region of France. His grandparents settled in San Francisco and opened a restaurant, with François making homemade wine for both family and restaurant patrons.

Two generations later, John now follows in his grandfather's footsteps. After obtaining a degree in culinary arts, John became a restaurateur; he, too, made wine on the side for his restaurant, as well as for his family and friends. Also a farmer and ranch developer, John's love of the land and his winemaking hobby led the couple and their family to where they are today.

Boëté's boutique wines are all estate grown with Cabernet Sauvignon and Cabernet Franc being the featured offerings. "John is a self-taught winemaker," explained Jana. "He has a passion for not only making a great wine, but also for producing the best grapes possible by working in the vineyard planting, pruning, thinning and harvesting to the end result of blending and bottling a beautiful wine." A relatively new and exciting wine that Boëté makes is its signature blend "Cheval Rouge." This true Bordeaux-style blend is made with Cabernet Sauvignon, Cabernet Franc and Merlot. The first release of the Cheval was such a hit that the Saunders had to triple production.

Winemaking continues to run in the family blood, as the fourth generation of Boëté/Saunders is involved in the business. Jesse (26), the Saunders' second oldest child, works at the winery full time and assists

> **WINE MYTH** "Wine is the nectar of the gods." — *Jana Saunders*

in nearly every aspect of the operation. Sam, two years Jesse's junior, also helps out, as does the youngest Dillon, that is, when he's home from college. The oldest—Justin (John's son and Jana's stepson)—lives in New York, but jumps in when he visits. "The best part of working with family is being able to work alongside our boys and watch them grow with the winery," shared Jana. "Our intention is to keep the business in the family for generations to come . . . hopefully."

Boëté Winery's tasting room is located in the Valley Hills Center, also home of both the popular Baja Cantina and Wagon Wheel restaurants. The tasting room can be hard to spot since the entrance to the center itself is on a turn; watch for a plant nursery, which is next door. Once you are in the parking lot, the tasting room will be to your right.

FEATURED WINE: Cabernet Sauvignon, Cabernet Franc and
Cabernet Franc Rosé
TASTING COST: $5
HOURS: Daily, 12 PM-5 PM
LOCATION: 7156A Carmel Valley Road, Carmel
PHONE: 831-625-5040
WEBSITE: www.boetewinery.com
GPS COORDINATES: 36.533972, -121.85014

Carmel

2 Chateau Julien Wine Estate

The classic French architecture and old-world ambiance of Chateau Julien Wine Estate set the mood for a wonderful tasting experience at this one-of-a-kind winery. The chateau itself appears as if it were built at least a lifetime ago or more; what visitors will not know, unless they ask or spot the small wall plaque out front, is that the noble estate was constructed in 1982.

We learned that Chateau Julien is family-owned and operated by Bob and Patty Brower, a couple who make frequent trips to France, especially to the country's Bordeaux wine region. We also learned, albeit after the fact, that it's not uncommon to find both Bob and Patty, very much hands-on owners, working at the estate on a daily basis. When we visited, we didn't put two-and-two together as staffer "Patty" answered our questions about the breathtaking tasting room and grounds.

Only later, when we called to confirm some information, did we learn that it was Patty Brower herself who actually had been our tour guide!

Tasting wine at Chateau Julien is an experience in and of itself. Entering through the wooden front doors and making your way around the formal entry, you'll find yourself in the "Great Hall," and what a hall it is. On one side of the room stands a large fireplace that rises several

(Photo courtesy of Chateau Julien)

stories high, and opposite is a towering stained-glass window featuring grapes and vines. The vaulted ceiling showcases two open-air loft windows (where the private vintner tasting room can be found), and regal wrought-iron chandeliers illuminate the room. But not to be outdone is the tasting experience; wine is not poured from behind a traditional tasting bar, but from an elegantly adorned table that sits directly in the center of the hall. We loved the experience of standing next to tasting room staff as they shared with us information about their wine offerings and answered our questions.

The outside grounds are just as impressive. A large glass-covered patio that easily can seat 100 visitors is located immediately outside the

Great Hall, and inviting cobblestone pathways and manicured gardens can be found just beyond. Picnics are encouraged, but pour only Chateau Julien wine, please.

Chateau Julien Wine Estate's winemaker is Bill Anderson, who has been with the winery since its very first vintage. A Stanford University graduate, Bill also holds a degree in enology from the University of California at Davis. Bill's strong desire for proprietary blends drove him to develop "Black Nova," a blend of Zinfandel and Syrah; this fruity-yet-dry full-bodied wine has hints of coffee, cedar, honeycomb and blueberry cobbler. In addition, this master winemaker has also created "La Conviviance," a blend of Merlot, Malbec and Cabernet Sauvignon. In 2010, the wine was awarded the "Best Blended Red Wine in the World" at the Ultimate Wine Challenge in New York.

WINE MYTH "You need to rinse your glass with water between tastes."
— *Bill Anderson*

One of the more interesting details about Chateau Julien is that it is the only full production winery in the county open daily to tours and tasting. Complimentary tours of the 16-acre estate are offered twice a day (Monday through Friday, 10:30 AM and 2:30 PM) and include a tour of the chateau, vineyard, barrel room and cellar. For those guests wanting to learn more—and to be spoiled rotten—they can treat themselves to the Le Petit Tour (one hour general tour, which includes tasting of select estate wines, $12) or the Winemaker's Tour, a 1.5 hour tour with the winemaker that includes an artisan cheese and fruit plate, tastings of premium wines and a souvenir wine glass ($50). The winery strongly recommends you call ahead to make reservations for the fee-based tours, as they fill quickly during the busy season. When entering the estate, parking is to your right and the chateau to your left.

FEATURED WINE: Merlot, Cabernet Sauvignon and Chardonnay
TASTING COST: $5
HOURS: Monday-Friday, 8 AM-5 PM; Saturday and Sunday, 11 AM-5 PM
LOCATION: 8940 Carmel Valley Road, Carmel
PHONE: 831-624-2600
WEBSITE: www.chateaujulien.com
GPS COORDINATES: 36.529044, -121.820855

Carmel-by-the Sea

3   Cima Collina

Annette Hoff is a woman. We realize this may be obvious, considering her first name. But it becomes more interesting when you add "winemaker" to the end of that statement. There are few female winemakers in the Mid-Coast region, and Annette is only one of two in this chapter.

Originally, Annette was studying at the University of California at Davis to become a veterinarian, but accidentally became a winemaker instead. "I realized the enology students were having way more fun than I was, so I took a few enology classes and then started working in a wine lab at Rodney Strong Vineyards," Annette shared. Over several years, she worked at two Napa wineries: Sterling Vineyards and Saintsbury Vineyards, where she confirmed her love for Pinot Noir. Following that love, in 1998 Annette traveled to New Zealand to study the varietal, working at various wineries. Within a few short months, though, Estancia Estates (Soledad) offered her a position as their Pinot Noir winemaker and it was here where Annette discovered the region's affinity for producing world-class Pinot Noir grapes. She has never left.

Well, she has never left Monterey County, that is. In 2004, grape grower Richard "Dick" Lumpkin, owner of Hilltop Ranch Vineyard, was looking for someone to help open a winery, someone with enthusiasm for artisan wine. His vineyard, located in the northwestern part of Monterey County near the Carmel Valley appellation, had provided grapes to other wineries, but up to that point, Dick had never made wine under his own label. He approached Annette; they struck an agreement and formed a partnership. The first release of wine under the new Cima Collina label (Cima Collina means "top hill" in Italian) came out in 2005.

When asked about her many experiences and the things she has learned in this business, Annette declared that the wonder and sense of mystery of the process never ceases to astound her. "I am constantly amazed at the wine grape's seemingly limitless capacity to produce a variety of flavors, aromas and other sensory characters. What other fruit—when made into wine—does that?"

Annette uses grapes from four different Monterey County vine-

yards: Chula Viña in Chualar Canyon, Cedar Lane Vineyards in Arroyo Seco, Tondre Grapefield in the Santa Lucia Highlands and Hilltop Ranch in the Carmel Valley. As mentioned earlier, the latter is Cima Collina's estate winery, owned by Dick Lumpkin. Retired from the telecommunications industry in 2005, Dick had planted the small vineyard of Pinot Noir and Pinot Gris grapes in 2002. He and his wife Ginny live on the property and tend to the grapes, with Dick being especially involved, loving every aspect of the vineyard and winery operations. According to Annette, "Dick has been known to work harvesting and sorting grapes at the winery into the wee hours of the morning and also helping with bottling. And although he is retired, he remains quite busy traveling for business and pleasure, spending time with his kids and grandkids—and sharing Cima Collina wines with friends and colleagues."

WINE MYTH "Winemakers make wine with their feet." — *Annette Hoff*

Undoubtedly, Annette's deep desire to showcase Cima Collina offerings as unique, food-friendly wines is evident in the winery's success. The smallness of the winery allows her to literally create her wine barrel by barrel. Of course her Pinot Noir is one of her favorites. She suggests that visitors to their inviting tasting room in Carmel-by-the-Sea should try the variety of Pinot Noirs they offer. "Most people are amazed at how different they all are," she said, with a smile. Another fun wine Annette created is called "Howlin' Good Red," a blend of red varietals. A portion of the proceeds from this wine is donated to the Monterey County SPCA. And yes, dogs are welcomed in their tasting room.

FEATURED WINE: Pinot Noir, Chardonnay, Meritage and Sauvignon Blanc
TASTING COST: $5, refunded with $40 purchase
HOURS: Thursday-Monday, 11 AM-6 PM
LOCATION: San Carlos between Ocean and 7th, Carmel-by-the-Sea
PHONE: 831-620-0645
WEBSITE: www.cimacollina.com
GPS COORDINATES: 36.55262, -121.921866

4 Galante Vineyards

Jack Galante's roots, and that of five generations of his family, run deep in the fertile soil of the Mid-Coast region. In 1902, Galante's great grandfather—James Frank Devendorf—was the first to file a sub-

division map in what would become the core village of downtown Carmel. In 1969, Jack's parents Jane and Clement Galante purchased a 700-acre cattle ranch in Carmel Valley, and in 1983 they planted their first grapevines. It wasn't until 1994 when Jack, who was selling his grapes to other wineries, built a winery of his own. A year later, Galante Vineyards released its first wine.

The ranch and winery continue to be a Galante-family enterprise. Jack is the president of the company, his wife Dawn

Galante Vineyards owner Jack Galante

is CFO and his five children are involved, including his oldest son John, who is studying agribusiness and viticulture at California Polytechnic State University. Jack's parents are also caught up in the excitement and are very supportive of Jack and the winery. Throw in the responsibility of maintaining a working ranch, and this posse is busy!

> **WINE MYTH** "If you look deep enough, all myths probably have some truth to them." — *Jack Galante*

Besides being president of the company, Jack and master winemaker Greg Vita oversee all winemaking aspects of the operation. "Greg has been making wine for Galante Vineyards since even before we opened the winery in 1994, and his dedication to excellence is reflected in the  ultra-premium wine that he produces," said Jack. "Galante Vineyards has always had a very simple philosophy: grow the finest grapes and let the fruit express itself in the wine." As evidence of his successful philosophy, according to Jack, his vineyard is recognized as one of the premier Cabernet Sauvignon producers in Monterey County and the entire state.

In talking with Jack, we could see his love of the Western lifestyle reflected in many ways, from his signature cowboy hat and authentic gentlemanly manner to his tasting-room motif and fun ranch-themed wine labels. One favorite is the ever-so-popular "Kick Ass Cabernet." The label bears a black-and-white photo of a mule with both back legs in a huge kick. The wine's descriptor states, "This untamed wine from our Carmel Valley Estate Vineyards has the familiar smell of open range cooking and camp coffee. You can't reason with a kickin' mule." There's also the name of their wine club—the Galante Wine Gang. "It's not a club, it's a gang," Jack said, with a laugh. The gang's logo is a caricature of Jack in full cowboy garb, including chaps, straddling a bottle of wine as if it were a horse trying to buck him off. To learn more about Jack, read his interview at **www.Wine-Wherever.com**.

The ranch and winery itself are located in Carmel Valley and open to the public only during special events, private tours and tastings. But don't dismay, as the Galante Vineyards tasting room is open daily.

Galante's Carmel-by-the-Sea tasting room

Located in Carmel-by-the Sea on Dolores Avenue between Ocean and 7th, the rustic Tudor-styled building is tucked into the right-hand corner of the Piccadilly Park complex. Besides being the first tasting room in downtown Carmel, the building doubles as a Western emporium; here you'll find whimsical cowboy items such as a leather cowboy boot chair (the toe of the boot is the ottoman) to logo'd Western merchandise to unique gifts made especially for Galante's customers. But we should point out that the Western motif is merely a fun complement to a wine that, well, kicks ass, to borrow a phrase from our most favorite Carmel cowboy! At Galante Vineyards, their motto is "Always drink upstream from the herd!"

FEATURED WINE: Cabernet Sauvignon, Pinot Noir, Sauvignon Blanc and Merlot
TASTING COST: $10 for 6-8 tastes, refundable with $50 purchase
HOURS: Sunday-Friday, 1 PM-6 PM; Saturday, 12 PM-6 PM
LOCATION: Dolores Avenue between Ocean and 7th, Carmel-by-the-Sea
PHONE: 831-624-3800
WEBSITE: www.galantevineyards.com
GPS COORDINATES: 36.554439, -121.922772

Carmel Valley

| 5 | # Heller Estate Organic Vineyards |

E ven though the wine at Heller Estate Organic Vineyards runs both white and red, this winery is all about green. As one of only a few

vineyards in California to be officially certified 100-per-cent organic by the Organic Certifiers in accordance with USDA-NOP National Organic Standards since 1996, the Heller's wonderful wine does the boasting for them.

Being green is not easy—it takes constant vigilance and attention to detail. For pest management, no pesticides are used. Instead, predator mites, ladybugs and predatory wasps (not the human-biting species) are employed to keep the undesirable pest population in check. The winery also utilizes the services of barn owls, providing comfy nesting boxes in their vineyards for their feathered night patrol. In return, the owls help keep gophers at bay. According to Gilbert Heller, viticulturist and co-owner of Heller along with his wife

Toby, gophers do a world of damage to the vineyards. "The gophers decimate the root system of the vine and that kills the vine," explained Gilbert.

Other aspects of farming organically, thus promoting a sustainable and healthy growing environment, involve soil and weed management. No herbicides are used; instead, leftover organic matter from the crushing and pressing of grapes is spread throughout the 120 acres of Cabernet Sauvignon, Merlot, Cabernet Franc, Chardonnay, Chenin Blanc and Pinot Noir vineyards, and weeds are controlled by planting cover crops—such as legumes, clover and vetch—in the vineyards. And the Hellers also ban the use of fossil fuels; they use biodiesel in all of their tractors. "Our goal is to produce the highest quality wines in the world, while leaving the smallest footprint on our precious earth," said

Gilbert. Production is about 25,000 cases annually.

Multi-millionaire William Durney, the owner of Carnation Seafood, planted the winery's original vineyard in 1968, releasing his first wine in 1976 under the Durney Family label. William passed away in the late 1980s, and the vineyard fell into disrepair. His widow Dorothy sold the vineyard to the Hellers in 1993.

Both Gilbert and Toby oversee the day-to-day operations of their winery and tasting room. Toby is also an internationally-known sculptress of large works. Many of her creations have become the inspiration for their wine labels; for example, the fifteen-foot-tall bronze sculpture titled "Dancers" that overlooks their vineyard is the idea behind their

"Dances on Your Palate" label. The same beautiful sculpture was cast for Heller's tasting room in Carmel Valley Village, but in aluminum instead of bronze. More sculptures can be found at the tasting room location in their outside "Secret Garden." Here you can relax in the garden and enjoy a glass of wine and view original Toby Heller works of art.

The Heller's tasting room is a treat, too. Built in the 1950s, the farm-style home was a residence and then a restaurant—the Country Kitchen—a popular Sunday brunch destination. The split barn-door entrance, rafter ceiling and old wood floors are reminiscent of the ranch-style feel. But wander into the rooms at the far side and you'll find black-and-white checkered floors and whimsical art pieces as well as items for sale. And don't be surprised to find tastings other than Heller's premium wine offerings: gourmet olive oils, vinegars and sauces often are available for visitors to enjoy.

FEATURED WINE: Chenin Blanc, Pinot Noir, Cabernet Sauvignon and Petit Verdot
TASTING COST: $7 standard, $15 premium
HOURS: Daily, 11 AM-5:30 PM
LOCATION: 69 W. Carmel Valley Road, Carmel Valley
PHONE: 800-659-6220
WEBSITE: www.hellerestate.com
GPS COORDINATES: 36.480745, -121.77355

6 | Joullian Vineyards

Raymond "Ridge" Watson, winemaker at Joullian Vineyards, is noted for saying his liquid creations are "serious wines that are fun to drink." And he should know, as Ridge is the backbone of Joullian; besides creating every wine Joullian has ever sold for nearly 30 years, it was Ridge who selected the vineyard site and cuttings for their unique "own-rooted" vineyard. He planted the 40-acre vineyard and helped design the winery. And if that wasn't enough, Ridge is also general manager.

When asked about the establishment of Joullian back in 1982,

(Photo courtesy of Ridge Watson)

Ridge answered that the founders—the Joullian and Sias families from Oklahoma—wanted "to create great estate grown Cabernet and Sauvignon Blanc near Carmel so that many restaurants could showcase our wines to visitors from around the world." He added that owner Richard "Dick" Sias personally planted the very first Zinfandel vine in Carmel Valley and went on to be known as "The Father of Carmel Valley Zinfandel." Sias is married to Jeannette Joullian—also an owner—but it was Jeannette and her brother Edward who were the winery's founders, hence the use of the family name for the business.

Joullian Vineyards' Ridge Watson

While the majority of Joullian's vineyards are planted with Cabernet Sauvignon, they also grow Zinfandel. "We create wines from our own-rooted vines, dormant fruitwood canes that are planted directly into the soil, not grafted onto other rootstock. By planting specially selected fruitwood, we can recreate the wines of pre-phylloxera (1860s)," explained Ridge. He added that most other vineyards graft desired varietal fruitwood onto rootstock selected for its resistance to disease, cold temperatures or other problems. Ridge emphasized that Joullian's fruitwood plantings come from vines carefully selected from famed vineyards such as Lytton Springs (Healdsburg), St. Peter's Church (Cloverdale) and Brandlin (Napa Valley).

For those not familiar with phylloxera, a quick recap of its history: North American grapes were mostly resistant to the damage that a native louse inhabiting their roots could cause. Unfortunately, American grape rootstock, unknowingly infested with phylloxera, was transplanted in Europe during the 1860s. That little North American louse quickly spread throughout much of the continent's nonresistant vineyards and literally wiped out the French wine industry. Today, phylloxera is kept under control with close monitoring, often in connection with the use of desired varietal fruitwood grafted onto disease-resistant rootstock.

Being in the wine industry has been Ridge's life-long dream. A Kansas City native, in the 1960s Ridge attended Stanford University and studied under famed wine merchant Dick Russ. He then spent more than three years with the Peace Corps, working for the National Potable Water Project in Thailand. There he met his wife D'Tim, a Thailand native educated in Australia. The two married in Carmel Valley in 1972, not realizing they would return ten years later when Ridge accepted the winemaker position at Joullian. During those intervening ten years, Ridge obtained a masters degree in food sciences with an emphasis in enology from California State University at Fresno. He apprenticed in Australia and the Bordeaux region of France.

WINE MYTH "European wines have fewer chemical additives than American wines." — *Ridge Watson*

Ridge has a right to be proud of his past and his present, as the wines of Joullian are stunning. When it comes to winemaking, one of his favorite experiences is, "Sunrise over the vineyard followed by a long distance phone call from a complete stranger wanting to order 'The best Cabernet I've ever had!'" Many agree, including the PGA: during the last 10 years, they have twice chosen Joullian Vineyards for their "Player's Wine" selection, the most recent occurring for the 2010 U.S. Open at Pebble Beach. It doesn't hurt that Ridge's brother is golf legend Tom Watson. To learn more about Ridge, read his interview at **www.WineWherever.com**.

The winery itself is open to the public only for special events. But don't dismay; their tasting room in Carmel Valley Village is open daily. Even though the tasting room is a tad tricky to find (heading south on Carmel Valley Road, watch for the Chevron Station then take the next right onto Village Drive—Joullian is directly to your left), you won't be disappointed. Their French provincial motif inside and out is a treat, just like their wine.

FEATURED WINE: Sauvignon Blanc, Chardonnay, Cabernet Sauvignon and Zinfandel
TASTING COST: $7
HOURS: Daily, 11 AM-5 PM
LOCATION: 2 Village Drive, Suite A, Carmel Valley
PHONE: 831-659-8100
WEBSITE: www.joullian.com
GPS COORDINATES: 36.479469, -121.732923

Carmel Valley

7 Parsonage Estate Winery

What do you get when you take a garbage man, quilt artist, three daughters, two sons-in-law, four young grandsons, a large dose of humor and the gumption to never give up on one's dream? You get the wonderful family behind Parsonage Estate Winery.

Bill Parsons, aka, former garbage man, current winery owner and self-admitted insane winemaker, has the world by its toes when it comes to creating amazing wines. But that wasn't always the case! When he and his wife Mary Ellen (the quilt artist) became partners in a Northern California vineyard in the 1980s, they had no way of knowing the venture would turn out to be a financial disaster. Determined to make their dream a reality, and learning from their mistake, Bill

Parsonage Estate owner Bill Parsons

attended viticulture and enology classes at the University of California at Davis. With his newfound knowledge, the couple made a go at the wine business again in 1998, this time planting their own vineyard.

The Parsons are proud of their success and have a right to be. Two years after planting their vineyard, they harvested their first small crop. This first release consisted of two varietals—125 cases of Syrah and 75 cases of a blend consisting of Cabernet, Merlot, Petit Verdot and Malbec. The entire lot sold out in four months, and hence, Parsonage Estate Winery became a reality. Not bad for a practically self-taught winemaker!

When asked about his inauspicious start in the wine industry, all Bill could do was laugh. "Momentary lapse of sanity," was his answer. Prior to getting into the business he now treasures, Bill spent time with the 5th Special Forces patrolling the jungles of Vietnam; worked undercover for U.S. Army Intelligence in Verona, Italy; earned a master's degree in journalism from Columbia University in New York; and worked as a staff writer for the *Carmel Pine Cone*. Bill had come to Carmel when offered a television reporter position at the NBC affiliate in Salinas, but the guy he was replacing decided to keep his job. Bill didn't learn of this until after he and Mary Ellen arrived, having traveled across the country in their VW bus. They decided to stay in Carmel—Bill secured a job in the waste management

> **WINE MYTH** "If the wine is of great character and depth of complexity, then the more I drink, the smarter and better looking I get!"
> — *Bill Parsons*

business where he worked as a general manager and then as a partner. "And the winemaker is still insane," Bill added, referring to himself. "After a 20-year career as a garbage man, I decided to go into a different aromatic enterprise and I've never regretted it." To read more of Bill's interview, go to **www.WineWherever.com**.

At Parsonage, family is important. "When we need extra help during harvest, bottling and special events, the entire family comes together to complete the work," shared Bill, noting that their middle daughter Ali is their office manager and her husband Frank is their vineyard manager, assistant winemaker and cellar manager. "And we named four estate reserve wines after our grandsons: Rocco Syrah, Bixby Petit Verdot, Dario Merlot and Tanner Cabernet Sauvignon," boasted a very proud grandfather, adding that all four boys are under the age of six. Now that would keep anyone busy!

Bill Parsons and son-in-law Frank Melicia

Not to be outdone by the crazy winemaker, Mary Ellen Parsons is an amazing artist—just take one look at her work in Parsonage's tasting room and you'll understand. A self-taught textile artist who began by making quilts in the late 1970s, Mary Ellen has won numerous awards and her work has been featured in many quilting books. But what is most interesting is her use of a high-resolution printing process called "giclee." We asked Mary Ellen about giclee (pronounced zhee-CLAY) after seeing her work hanging throughout the tasting room—what looks like a quilt is actually a giclee print. "A giclee is a super-high resolution art image printed with archival pigments on either canvas or paper," she explained, noting that it is reputed to be the longest lived, non-fading form of print making. Being very supportive of local artisans, the Parsons also host a large gallery adjacent to their tasting room that is not to be missed, with a glass of Parsonage Estate wine in hand, of course!

FEATURED WINE: Syrah, Cabernet Sauvignon, Merlot and Petit Verdot
TASTING COST: $7, waived with purchase of $50 or more
HOURS: Daily, 11 AM–5 PM
LOCATION: 19 E. Carmel Valley Road, Carmel Valley
PHONE: 831-659-2215
WEBSITE: www.parsonagewine.com
GPS COORDINATES: 36.477818, -121.72869

8 Talbott Vineyards

The Robert Talbott name is synonymous with the finer things in life. Founders of the Robert Talbott Tie Company, Robert Talbott Sr. and his wife Audrey also loved wine and discovered exceptional offerings during their many trips to Europe in the 1950s and '60s in search of silk for their new neckwear line. With young son Robert "Robb" Talbott Jr. in tow, the couple grew to especially love and appreciate wine from the Burgundy region of France.

Prior to their forays to Europe, the three Talbotts moved to Carmel from Connecticut in 1950, where the family established the luxury tie company. Audrey sewed the ties by hand and Robert Sr. literally sold them by hand, traversing the entire California coast. Young Robb helped, too. After high school, he went to college in Colorado where he majored in fine art. While in the mile-high state, Robb raced motorcycles and started a business buying, restoring and then selling antique

cars and trucks. In the early 1970s, he returned home and resumed work in the family business.

A self-proclaimed nature lover, Robb built a cabin on a remote piece of land high above the valley floor. It was on this land that Robb decided to plant a vineyard in 1982. Locals warned him that the mountain would be too difficult to plant and too cold for grapes, but Robb

---

WINE MYTH "Aged wines taste better." — *Robb Talbott*

---

proved them wrong. With pure determination and sheer grit, and using a 12-pound sledgehammer to break the massive boulders that littered the area, Robb negotiated the steep mountainside and planted the now famous Diamond T Vineyard, naming it in honor of an antique Diamond T commercial truck he had once restored.

That same year, Robb, along with his father, founded Robert Talbott Vineyards, now known as Talbott Vineyards. At first, they used grapes from the Diamond T Vineyard and also sourced from the Sleepy Hollow Vineyard in the Santa Lucia Highlands. It wasn't until 1994 that the Talbotts purchased Sleepy Hollow, thus making their wines an all-estate brand.

Today, Robb wears two hats, one as the hands-on proprietor of Talbott Vineyards, the other as the chairman of the board of the Robert Talbott Tie Company. Talbott's winemaker is none other than Dan Karlsen; with three decades in the business, Karlsen has worked for such outstanding wineries as Dehlinger (Sebastopol), Domaine Carneros (Napa) and Chalone (Soledad). Having direct access to two of the most notable vineyards in the industry while at Talbott, Karlsen has created amazing Pinot Noirs and Chardonnays.

Talbott Vineyards has two tasting rooms. The primary tasting room, which is open daily, is located in Carmel Valley Village. A former home and later a Thai restaurant, the building hosts a 35-foot-long tasting bar, seating area with a homelike ambiance and an outdoor patio with plenty of tables. In one corner hangs Robb's old red bike: a former cycling enthusiast, Robb once raced until a crash did him in and he retired from the sport. Behind the massive tasting bar is a collection of old cars and toys—gifts from his father who would bring them back from his many trips overseas. The winery itself is located on River Road in Salinas, where the second tasting room can be found. It is interesting to note that Robb designed the winery building.

CARMEL VALLEY TASTING ROOM
FEATURED WINE: Chardonnay and Pinot Noir
TASTING COST: $7.50 to $16
HOURS: Daily, 11 AM-5 PM
LOCATION: 53 W. Carmel Valley Road, Carmel Valley
PHONE: 831-659-3500
WEBSITE: www.talbottvineyards.com
GPS COORDINATES: 36.480115, -121.73677

WINERY TASTING ROOM
HOURS: Friday-Sunday, 11 AM-5 PM
LOCATION: 1380 River Road, Salinas
PHONE: 831-659-3000
WEBSITE: www.talbottvineyards.com
GPS COORDINATES: 36.498192, -121.5013

9 Scheid Vineyards

Scheid Vineyards Winery is the largest independent grape grower and producer of wine in all of Monterey County, even though Scheid releases a mere 10,000 cases per year under its own estate label. The remaining 98 percent of their grapes from their ten estate vineyards are purchased by other wineries. Of those wineries, as many as 50—which Scheid refers to as "partners in wine"—utilize Scheid's mammoth production facility via custom-crush arrangements. At the end of a harvest, it is not uncommon for the facility to be operating at full capacity, with six million gallons crushed and fermenting in tanks.

Marta Kraftzeck, Scheid's cellar operations supervisor—or as she calls herself, "the production gal"—took us on an exclusive behind-the-

Scheid Vineyard's Greenfield tasting room

scenes tour of their massive operation. Scheid is, by far, the biggest production facility we visited during our research for this book. Giant stainless-steel tanks towered over us as we walked row after row. Marta then took us upstairs to the catwalk, where we looked down upon a sea of sparkling tanks. She led us to an empty tank where we peered into the depths of the behemoth container. Even though it was empty, the vastness inside was extreme. Just think about it: a 19,000 gallon stainless-steel tank holds up to 8,000 cases of wine, the equivalent of 96,000 bottles or nearly a half million glasses. Scheid has 356 tanks ranging in size from 350 gallons to 132,000 gallons, adding up to a capacity of 6 million gallons, or the equivalent of 2.5 million cases. Those are some impressive numbers.

Alfred "Al" Scheid founded Scheid Vineyards in 1972 with partner E. F. Hutton Company. Besides overseeing the vineyard business, Al—the perpetual entrepreneur—founded two biotechnology companies, serving as CEO at both. In 1988, he bought out partner E. F. Hutton, becoming sole owner of Scheid. He also founded the California Association of Winegrape Growers and the Monterey County Vintners and Growers Association, the county's main winery organization. CEO of Scheid until 2002, Al turned the operation over to son Scott and daughter Heidi. Al is still involved in the family business, manning the helm as chairman of the board.

During the 1970s and throughout the '80s, Scheid sold all of its grapes to other wine labels. In the early 1990s the family released the first wine under its own label, a 1989 Cabernet Sauvignon. The rest is history, according to Heidi. "We produce 30 different Scheid labels, and yes, that's a lot!" she said, noting that their winemaker—Dave Nagengast—is like a kid in a candy store when it comes to selecting grapes from Scheid's 4,500 acres of premium fruit. "Dave is affectionately known as the 'gentle giant,' but is a bulldog when it comes to quality.

He works hard at choosing specific vineyard rows for the Scheid label, keeping all of the lots separate in the winery, and then blending to his heart's content to come up with the final composition."

As senior vice president, Heidi is involved in all areas of the operation, from the vineyard to the winery to their two tasting rooms (Greenfield and Monterey). But her favorite part of the job is when she and the staff conduct their "in-house tastings" for the Scheid brand. Nagengast and his winemaking team put together sample bottles for the staff to taste and comment upon before coming up with the final blends. Heidi picks up the story from there: "These meetings start off

---

WINE MYTH "Cork is the best closure for wines!" — *Heidi Scheid*

---

a little bit serious, but quickly turn into in-depth discussion, hilarious commentary and some of the best descriptions of the wine you'll *never* see in print!" she shared. "For example, we dubbed our 'Odd Lot White' wine as the perfect hot tub wine because, in the words of one of our guys, 'This wine should only be consumed naked . . . no clothes al-

lowed!'" Heidi did confide that that particular description never made it to the back of the bottle.

Heidi continues: "I guess that leads to another favorite aspect about what I do; the wine industry is known for its camaraderie and kinship, and this stems from the fact that everyone genuinely loves what they're doing and feels privileged to be making such a cool product. There's no better feeling than sitting around a table and tasting wines with people who love wine as much as you do!"

That's what you'll find at both of Scheid's tasting rooms: they love their wine and their visitors. At the main production facility in Greenfield, the tasting room is very welcoming, as are the staffers who are all eager to please. One special detail that the female half of this writing team loved was discovered in the restroom: instead of paper towels, Scheid offers individual soft terry cloth towels. Outside, with a delightful glass of wine in hand, be sure to head around back to the "Demonstration Vineyard." In this special acre, visitors can learn about the art of grape growing.

Scheid's second tasting room is located on Cannery Row in Monterey, and its chic wine-lounge décor is very different than its Greenfield counterpart. Here the staff is equally as accommodating and will welcome you to relax in leather chairs

Scheid Vineyards' Cannery Row tasting room

next to a modern stone fireplace while enjoying your taste. Several large flat-screen televisions are found throughout, showing events and videos about Scheid and the Greenfield facility. And yes, ladies, you'll also find real towels in the restrooms!

FEATURED WINE: Chardonnay, Pinot Noir, Riesling and Petite Sirah
TASTING COST: Greenfield Tasting Room: $5; Cannery Row Tasting Room: $10. Fees are refunded with a wine purchase.

WINERY AND TASTING ROOM
HOURS: Daily, 11 AM-5 PM
LOCATION: 1972 Hobson Avenue, Greenfield
PHONE: 831-386-0316
WEBSITE: www.scheidvineyards.com
GPS COORDINATES: 36.275504, -121.186607

CANNERY ROW TASTING ROOM
HOURS: Daily, 11 AM-7 PM
LOCATION: 751 Cannery Row, Monterey
PHONE: 831-656-9463
WEBSITE: www.scheidvineyards.com
GPS COORDINATES: 36.616594, -121.900967

10 Sycamore Cellars

R obert "Robbie" Madsen, co-owner of Sycamore Cellars, has been in the wine business since he was a young teen. A high school sophomore in 1963, Robbie's first job was working for winery manager Jack Farrior at Paul Masson Winery (see page 144). "Paul Masson and Mirrasou were the first large vineyards to come to the Salinas Valley," Robbie said. "Jack made me start at the bottom and I loved every aspect of growing grapes. In 1965, Paul Masson started their winery in Soledad. Jack had me involved with that, also." Jack more than likely saw great potential in the young man and asked him to help establish Monterey Farming Corporation in 1972 (now known as Scheid Vineyards, page 37). Robbie worked there until 1981, developing vineyards.

As Robbie was honing his skills, another story that had begun a few years earlier was developing in the valley. In the 1950s, Harry

(Photo courtesy of Tobías López)

Kuchta bought a 200-acre ranch in Arroyo Seco, which originally had been a turkey farm. Working as a dairyman in Gonzales, Harry had purchased the ranch in hopes of someday starting his own dairy and creating a great livelihood for his young family. In 1956, he bought 100 head of dairy cows and together he, his wife Carmen and children did well. They also grew alfalfa, oat hay, fruits and vegetables. But as the years went on, Harry had to let his cattle go because he lost his "free help"—his boys went into the armed services. Little did Harry know that grape growers considered his property prime grape-growing land.

(Photo courtesy of Tobías López)

Harry's property was situated in a long valley in the most westerly part of the Santa Lucia Highlands—which is now the upper Arroyo Seco appellation. Growers wanted to buy the land and develop it into vineyards. Uncertain about the offers, Harry talked to his son-in-law Robbie Madsen who was married to his oldest daughter Barbara. Robbie stepped in and worked out growing deals, the biggest being with wine giant Kendall Jackson (Sonoma County). Now under contract and with that oh-so-important capital investment in their pockets, Robbie and the crew planted 25 acres of grapes, eventually expanding to 60. Other wineries began purchasing grapes, too. With the dedication and hard work of Harry, his son Dennis, his son-in-law the late Marvin Tavernetti (married to younger daughter Kathy) and Robbie, his other son-in-law, their newly founded Arroyo Seco Canyon Vineyard became a great success.

It wasn't until 2009 that the family began to create wine under their own label. Robbie considers himself and Dennis the unofficial winemakers at Sycamore Cellars. But they do utilize the services of a winemaking consultant, who happens to be a good friend of Robbie's—none other than Dan Karlsen. The Karlsen name is synonymous with fine winemaking in this region. Dan has worked for some of the greats, including Dehlinger Winery (Sonoma County), Chalone (Soledad) and can now be found as the general manager and winemaker for Talbott Winery (see page 34). "Dan has been instrumental in helping us get our wines off and running," Robbie said. When it comes to their offerings, Sycamore's leaders include Cabernet Sauvignon and Syrah.

Now in his early 90s, Harry rules the roost on the family ranch, which hosts the winery and tasting room. Four generations live on their ranch, beginning with Harry and extending down to his great grand-children. Even though he's not involved that much, "Harry is still a part

of it," Robbie mused. When asked about family and the future of Sycamore Cellars, Robbie confided: "My hope is to pass this on to the next generation, my sons Harry and Matt, plus the loves of my life— niece Emily [Kathy's daughter] and my

(Photo courtesy of Tobías López)

granddaughter Julia." To learn more about Robbie and his family, read his interview at **www.WineWherever.com**.

Sycamore Cellars is located approximately 12 miles west of the town of Greenfield. The drive to the winery will take you through roll-ing hills followed by steeper canyons; you might find yourself thinking that there is no way a winery could survive out here. But when you round the last corner before the driveway entrance, you'll be greeted by acres and acres of vineyards.

Once you've arrived at the tasting room, be sure to take in the view of the shale-faced mountains just across the valley; the stark beau-ty of the white shale is hard to miss. And don't overlook the fountain. On closer inspection, you will find a frog on top enjoying a bath. "We have lots of frogs around here. My wife put it up there for fun and the kids like it," Robbie said, with a laugh.

FEATURED WINE: Cabernet Sauvignon, Chardonnay, Pinot Noir and Syrah
TASTING COST: Complimentary
HOURS: Saturday, Sunday and holidays, 12 PM-5 PM
LOCATION: 45185 Arroyo Seco Road, Greenfield
PHONE: 831-674-5760
WEBSITE: www.thesycamorecellars.com
GPS COORDINATES: 36.271058, -121.392742

Monterey

11 A Taste of Monterey

A Taste of Monterey is just that—a taste of Monterey. The business showcases all the member wineries in the Monterey County Vintners and Growers Association (MCVGA), thus making it a regional wine visitor's center. Their motto is "Great taste comes with the territory."

Though the center itself is less than 20 years old, the large Cannery Row building where it is located (now a unique shopping mall) has an interesting back story. From 1910-1916, the site was home to the Chinese Monterey Fish Canning Company, becoming the Monterey Canning Company in 1918. It was one of many busy and productive sardine-canning factories that lined the main road, known back then

Monterey tasting room (Photo courtesy of A Taste of Monterey)

as "Ocean View Avenue." It wasn't until 1958 that Ocean View Avenue was renamed "Cannery Row" by the city to honor favorite son John Steinbeck and his famous novel by the same name. But even Steinbeck's touch couldn't save the sardine industry; over-fishing decimated the sardine population and the last cannery standing closed its doors in 1973.

A few years later, the defunct and abandoned building was turned into a popular tourist destination, and in 1989 Paul Masson Tasting Room and Museum was opened in the same section of the building that A Taste of Monterey now occupies. Today, the 4,000 square-foot regional wine visitor's center, located on the second floor, should be a required stop for its view alone: No other tasting room in the county

is literally perched over Monterey Bay. Considering that the entire ocean-facing side of the tasting room is wall-to-wall glass, with tables and seating areas throughout, it's the best bay panorama/tasting experience pairing of all the wineries featured in this book. The center also features one of the greatest selections in the area of wine-related gifts mixed with top-quality kitchen-ware available for purchase. And we mustn't forget the center's dedication to showcasing the history of winemaking in Monterey County—in addition to the many photos and items on display, its historical masterpiece is the actual 1897 wine press Paul Masson himself used at his winery back in the day (see page 144).

Without a doubt, visitors come here for both the view and huge selection of wine tasting options. According to Ken Rauh, director of operations for A Taste of Monterey, the center proudly caters to upwards of 100,000 guests annually at their Cannery Row location, as well as at their sister center in Salinas (across from the National Steinbeck Center). Representing 85 wineries and seven varying appellations, this highly unique business does an impressive job indeed at presenting, highlighting, educating and promoting the wines of Monterey County.

As previously mentioned, a sister wine center is located in Old Town Salinas, near the National Steinbeck Center and just blocks from

Salinas tasting room

Steinbeck's boyhood home. Located inside a building that dates from the 1890s, the historic structure was once the home of the Pia family. "The family operated it as a market deli for years," shared Ken. "There's a story that Frank Sinatra loved the Italian salami they sold and had stopped by on a trip from or to Los Angeles. He grabbed some salami and a beer and had a picnic right there on the floor of the deli. They had to tell him he couldn't do that!" Even though this tasting room doesn't boast the view of its flagship store, it makes up for it with its gorgeous and chic barn-style wooden interior offset by an old brick wall. If it's not busy, ask staffers if you can peek in the basement, and while down there, be sure to also ask them to share with you a little of Salinas' fascinating underground history.

FEATURED WINE: Host myriad Monterey County wines
TASTING COST: $5-20

CANNERY ROW BAY VIEW TASTING ROOM
HOURS: Daily, 11 AM-6 PM
LOCATION: 700 Cannery Row, Ste. KK, Monterey
PHONE: 831-646-5446
WEBSITE: www.tastemonterey.com
GPS COORDINATES: 36.61618, -121.900294

SALINAS WINE CELLAR AND TASTING ROOM
HOURS: Monday-Saturday, 11 AM-5 PM; closed Sundays
LOCATION: 127 Main Street, Salinas
PHONE: 831-751-1980
WEBSITE: www.tastemonterey.com
GPS COORDINATES: 36.676796, -121.655307

Monterey

12 Bargetto Winery

Even though Bargetto's main winery is in Soquel, their Cannery Row tasting room, found in Monterey, is worth an extra mention. (Please see page 211 for the entire story and history behind one of the region's oldest family-owned wineries.)

Open daily, the main entrance to the tasting room is located off the courtyard leading to the Bubba Gump Shrimp Company, a favorite restaurant stop for multitudes of tourists who flood Cannery Row during the travel season. There is also a back entrance from within the indoor mall.

Entering Bargetto from either direction, visitors are greeted by a nearly 20-foot long tasting bar. Behind the bar are the tasting room's offerings, including their best-selling wine—a stunning Pinot Grigio. More wine can be found in gorgeous display cases throughout the large tasting room and gift shop, to-

Bargetto Winery's Monterey tasting room

gether with a vast array of high-end kitchen articles, Italian porcelain, wine-related items and gourmet food selections.

Cannery Row can be overwhelming to navigate especially during the busy tourist season, so when you look for Bargetto Winery, watch for a giant bay window facing the outdoor courtyard. You'll be glad you did, as the refuge inside promises delights galore, and the Bargetto staff will take great care of you and your guests.

FEATURED WINE: Chardonnay, Pinot Grigio, Pinot Noir and Merlot
TASTING COST: $5 for five tastes
HOURS: Daily, 11 AM-7 PM
LOCATION: 700-G Cannery Row, Monterey
PHONE: 831-373-4053
WEBSITE: www.bargetto.com
GPS COORDINATES: 36.61618, -121.900294

13 Pierce Ranch Vineyards

If you're in the mood for Spanish and Portuguese wines, then be sure to check out Pierce Ranch Vineyards. This small operation offers a most unusual and exciting selection of varietals common to the Iberian Peninsula region of extreme southwest Europe, which encompasses Portugal, Spain, Gibraltar, Andorra and a small portion of France. But Pierce Ranch's vineyards are found half a world away from Europe, in the San Antonio Valley region of southern Monterey County.

Their premium estate-grown grapes include such off-the-beaten-path varietals as Portugal's Touriga, a small red wine grape. In Portugal and other parts of the world, Touriga is actually two varietals—Touriga Nacional and Touriga Francesa—but because of crazy U.S. labeling

laws, only the generic "Touriga" name can be used in the United States. Pierce Ranch Vineyards proudly specializes in Touriga Nacional, Portugal's finest indigenous varietal. Another noted favorite is the varietal Albariño, a white grape from northwest Spain and northwest Portugal (also referred to as "Alvarinho"). Regarding this grape's origins, legend has it that 12th century monks took Riesling clones from the Alsace region of France to the Iberian Peninsula and planted them, coining the new varietal name. But the earliest records show that Riesling grapes date only as far back as the 15th century—not the 12th—so it's anyone's guess which clones the monks actually used.

Pierce Ranch Vineyards encompasses 30 acres in the Santa Lucia Range and is located about 14 miles from the Pacific Ocean and 25 miles from Paso Robles in San Luis Obispo County. This isolated and sparsely populated part of Monterey County is experiencing a boom of activity as vineyards are popping up all over, especially along Jolon Road. Those familiar with the history of this region know that one of the earliest vineyards in the western U.S. was planted here in the 1770s at Mission San Antonio de Padua. The third California mission founded by Father Junipero Serra, San Antonio de Padua is still standing and open to the public. But for wine buffs, better yet is that a solitary Mis-

sion varietal grapevine from the original vineyard can be found near the mission's well. There's only one hitch if you want to see the grapevine for yourself: the mission is on the grounds of Fort Hunter Liggett, an active military base and the nation's largest U.S. Army Reserve command post. (To learn more, especially about rules regarding access, go to Side Trips, page 78.)

Just like Father Serra, the Pierce family realized the land's rich and fertile potential. In 1998, owners Bill and Gail Pierce purchased the property, planting their vineyards a year later. "We sold fruit in our first couple of production years, and we still sell a good amount of Petite

Sirah every year," said Josh Pierce, the couple's son and also the general manager of Pierce Ranch Vineyards. The family released its first wine under their own label in 2005.

> **WINE MYTH** "This is always a hopelessly romantic endeavor."
> — *Josh Pierce*

Josh's roots in this region run deep, as the maternal side of his family settled here in 1848. Born in Salinas, Josh grew up in the area, but never had his sights set on the wine industry. With a bachelor's degree in English from Stanford, and then a master's in literature from San Francisco State University, Josh worked in the publishing industry for many years before returning to Monterey to help with the new family business. Prior to his return, a fateful trip to Portugal sealed his passion for wine: "There, in the northern part of the country, I ran across Albariño for the first time, and that started me down the track of trying to learn more about Portuguese and then eventually Spanish wines. When my parents started the vineyard, I was always a proponent of experimenting with things from the Iberian Peninsula, and I still am a proponent for things experimental in general."

You don't have to head south to enjoy Pierce Ranch Vineyards wine. Their tasting room is located a block up from Cannery Row on Wave Street. Built in 1915, the home, which is now the tasting room, was originally that of a cannery manager. Inside, you'll find an inviting L-shaped bar with barstools, and outside, delightful garden seating, either of which makes a perfect setting for sipping a glass of Pierce Ranch wine.

FEATURED WINE: Albariño, Tempranillo, Touriga and Petite Sirah
TASTING COST: $5 refunded with purchase
HOURS: Sunday and Monday, 12 PM-6:30 PM; Tuesday and Wednesday, 1 PM-6:30 PM; Thursday-Saturday, 12 PM-8 PM
LOCATION: 499 Wave Street, Monterey
PHONE: 831-372-8900
WEBSITE: www.piercevineyards.com
GPS COORDINATES: 36.613148, -121.89936

Monterey

14 Ventana

Ventana has been an integral part of the wine industry in Monterey County for more than 30 years. Owned by a small group of local growers, with a collective knowledge of this region that spans generations, Ventana makes their own wine and sources their fruit to other wineries. They take great pride regarding the latter, stating that Ventana has the most award-winning single vineyard in America.

Ventana is named after the Ventana Wilderness, which is part of the nearby Los Padres National Forest. The original federal wilderness

Ventana's Monterey tasting room

designation occurred in 1969 and, as of 2002, encompasses more than 240,000 acres, including the Santa Lucia Mountains. Barbara Pluth, Ventana's tasting room manager at their Monterey location, explained even earlier origins of the name Ventana: "When the Spanish explorer Gaspar de Portolà came ashore in Big Sur in 1769, he proceeded inland through what is now called the Ventana Wilderness and peered into the fertile Salinas Valley through a gap formed by the Arroyo Seco Canyon. They called the gap 'La Ventana,' the Spanish word for 'window.'"

Doug Meador is the founder of Ventana. A legend in the world of California wine and viticulture research, In 1974 Doug planted a range of varietals he knew would do well. Today, the winery has two vineyards totaling 440 acres—the aforementioned award-winning Ventana Vineyard as well as the Le Mistral Vineyard. The winery is a leader when it comes to sustainable agricultural practices. Visit its website to

Ventana's Soledad tasting room

learn more about its farming protocol.

Ventana has two very different and distinct tasting rooms, one in Monterey and the other in Soledad. Their Monterey tasting room is open daily and is a fun stop, especially if you like history. A part of the nearly century-old Ryan Ranch homestead, the tasting room, according to Ventana staffers, was most likely an added bedroom section to this historic home. The well-known Tarpy's Roadhouse Restaurant also occupies a portion of the 1917 home. A wonderful place to eat, the restaurant offers complimentary corkage of Ventana wines.

Ventana's other tasting room is located in Soledad and sits adjacent to their winery operation. Open only on weekends, the tasting bar has that totally rustic feel, especially when you look up to the ceiling and see sunlight coming back through the old barn's wooden shingles!

FEATURED WINE: Chardonnay, Pinot Noir, Sauvignon Blanc and Syrah
TASTING COST: $5.00, refunded with $15 purchase

MONTEREY TASTING ROOM
HOURS: Daily, 11 AM-5 PM
LOCATION: 2999 Monterey-Salinas Hwy. #10, Monterey
PHONE: 831-372-7415
WEBSITE: www.ventanawines.com
GPS COORDINATES: 36.581866, -121.830601

WINERY TASTING ROOM
HOURS: Saturday and Sunday, 11 AM-5 PM
LOCATION: 38740 Los Coches Road, Soledad
PHONE: 831-372-7415
WEBSITE: www.ventanawines.com
GPS COORDINATES: 36.361042, -121.306915

15 Pessagno Winery

Pessagno Winery, located on River Road in Salinas, is a popular stop for wine lovers and wine enthusiasts alike. Even though the winery and tasting room opened their doors to the public in 2004, the wine-making history of this family goes back nearly 40 years.

The inspiration for owner Steve Pessagno was his maternal grandfather Anthony Escover. Steve recalls his grandfather introducing him to the craft of winemaking on the family's Santa Clara ranch in 1974. "My grandfather was a huge role model for me. My cousin Dave and I would spend every summer in our youth at his ranch. He taught us farming, mechanical work, hunting and cooking. He also made his own wine for a hobby, which is what influenced me to create my own wine," Steve reminisced.

Steve chose mechanical engineering as his career path, where he studied and helped develop alcohol combustion engines. In his spare time, he made wine in his garage. Wanting to learn more about wine-

making, Steve worked a crush at Kirigin Cellars (see page 99) in 1982, and that is where he became hooked on opening his own winery. Upon obtaining a degree in enology from California State University at Fresno in 1986, Steve found himself vice president and winemaker for Jekel Vineyards (Monterey County). In 1991, he became winemaker for Lockwood Vineyards (also Monterey County), a position he held

until 2004 when he left to fulfill his dream of opening his own winery.

Pessagno Winery is a family affair, mainly of the manly kind. Steve's four sons have all worked in the family business. Eldest is Anthony who works full time at the winery and tasting room, while his younger brothers Stephen, Robert and John attend college. Because the property has four small Pinot Noir vineyards—each named for one of his sons—Steve created a specialty blend he

calls "Four Boys Vineyard." It's a popular wine, according to Steve who added: "Combined, the four vineyards are about 3.5 acres, which enables us to produce about 200-300 cases annually."

Both Steve and Anthony showed us different parts of the 15-acre winery complex. Steve took us to the winery's charming Highlands House, a fully furnished two bedroom/one bath home available for reservation. Just steps away from the winery, the home features a fully equipped kitchen and private backyard. "When our customers leave for the day, it is quiet and peaceful," Steve said. "Just imagine having this place all to yourself!" But what Steve loved the most was the home's man-made pond. "We call it 'Duck Pond,'" Steve smiled while pointing out several favorite resident ducks. When asked about feathered visitors, Steve said, "Our favorite migratory birds that visit are the Can-

> **WINE MYTH** "Cab is king and Pinot Noir is feminine."
> — Anthony Pessagno

ada geese because they make such a big racket when coming through."

A tour of the tasting room and surrounding grounds with Anthony was just as much fun. The tasting room—called the "Lucia Tasting and Event Room"—used to be one of the 30 dairies that blanketed the area back in the 1920s and '30s. According to Anthony, a Swiss-Italian family by the name of Selva in 1900 established the dairy that is now the home of Pessagno Winery; the tasting room was the dairy barn and milking facility. "If you look here," Anthony said, pointing to large marred markings in the cement floor that skirts the hardwood flooring, "you'll see cow skids." Sans the cow skids, the expansive tasting room is drop dead gorgeous, with its stately tasting bar, welcoming black leather barstools, and the stunning stained glass window—labeled "Pessagno"—over French doors leading to the vineyards. Just outside, you'll find a large barbeque and picnic area shaded by 40-year-old walnut trees.

FEATURED WINE: Chardonnay, Pinot Noir, Zinfandel and Port
TASTING COST: $5-$15 for reserve
HOURS: Monday-Thursday, 11 AM-4 PM; Friday-Sunday, 11 AM-5 PM
LOCATION: 1645 River Road, Salinas
PHONE: 831-675-9463
WEBSITE: www.pessagnowines.com
GPS COORDINATES: 36.479858, -121.48459

16 Hahn Winery

Just as their slogan says, Hahn Winery produces "wines of Monterey distinction." Located in the heart of Monterey County, their vineyards are nestled in the spirited foothills of the Santa Lucia Highlands, and the spectacular hillside view from their tasting room and large deck balcony showcases the lush Salinas Valley. Distinction definitely reigns supreme, and for good reason.

Back in the 1970s, owners and married couple Nicolaus ("Nicky")

and Gaby Hahn came to California from Europe, pining for the perfect place to grow premium varietal grapes. They settled in Monterey's highlands, purchasing two ranches-turned-vineyards— the Smith and Hook ranches. Neighboring properties, the Smith Ranch had once been a horse ranch, while cattle were the focus for many generations at the Hook Ranch. In 1980, the Hahns released their first varietal to much acclaim—a Cabernet Sauvignon—under the label of "Smith & Hook Winery." They sold their wine from an old barn on the ranch, using a former tack room as their first tasting room.

Today, the winery boasts of 960 acres of grapes in Monterey County and another 300 acres south in Paso Robles. Many of their vineyards are named after family members; for example, the Doctor's Vineyard is named for their daughter Caroline, a large-animal veterinarian in Scotland. The Hahns sell their wine under eight different and distinct labels, including one featuring a vibrant rooster, their official mascot. In German, "hahn" means "rooster."

WINE MYTH "The best wines come with the steepest prices."
— *Bill Leigon, president of Hahn Family Wines*

Their winemaker is Paul Clifton. Paul joined Hahn in 2003 after finishing a postgraduate degree in viticulture and enology in New Zealand. A native of Monterey Bay, Paul worked as an assistant winemaker for several local wineries before landing at Hahn. Paul's a busy guy, so you'll probably not see him during your visit, but more than likely you'll meet his dog Parker. A German Shorthaired Pointer, Parker is Hahn's official canine greeter and will happily escort you to the tasting room.

One of the major reasons for the Hahn's success is their long-standing commitment to sustainability and green business practices. Hahn Winery was the first in the region to become green certified by the Monterey Bay Area Green Business Program, and in 2008 they received Sustainability in Practice (SIP) certification by the Central Coast Vineyard Team. SIP certification confirms a winery's commitment to farming practices that protect both human and natural resources. But one of Nicky's proudest achievements is when he spurred the pioneering efforts that led to the creation of one of the nation's most exciting appellations—the Santa Lucia Highlands AVA.

The Hahns are good stewards of the land and of the people. A Swiss citizen, Nicky grew up in both the U.S. and Europe. He studied economics and his career in the financial world had him working in Paris, London and New York, eventually ending up as the chairman of an international software development company. Gaby earned law degrees in both France and Germany, but her true love is art. An avid supporter of the arts in Monterey County, Gaby founded an art appreciation unit in the local school district. But the primary topic for her art can be found on the couple's 50,000-acre farm in Northern Kenya, Africa, where they reside part time. Here on "Mugie Ranch," they built a school for Kenyan children, established a farm and created a wild animal conservancy that focuses on endangered black rhinos. Sales of their Huntington wine label goes directly into a scholarship fund for the higher education of Kenyan children.

A visit to Hahn Winery is a must, especially since they are one of only a few wineries in the county that does not charge to taste. Turning onto the property, you'll drive 1.5 miles up the hill to the tasting room, which will be to your right. Once you park under the stately coastal live

 oaks, walk to the rear of the yellow building, as the entrance to the tasting room faces the gorgeous view of both the Salinas Valley and Pinnacles National Monument in the distance. Once inside, you'll be pampered by some of the friendliest tasting room staff in the business, including assistant manager Jay Olund. Be sure to ask him about the money tree behind the counter. "We guilt visitors into donating foreign money," Olund said, laughing. The winery encourages picnicking on its expansive deck, along with a bottle or two of their wine. And not to worry—Parker will help with any leftovers!

FEATURED WINE: Pinot Noir, Cabernet Sauvignon, Chardonnay and Syrah
TASTING COST: Complimentary
HOURS: Monday-Thursday, 11 AM-4 PM; Friday-Sunday, 11 AM-5 PM
LOCATION: 37700 Foothill Road, Soledad
PHONE: 831-678-4555
WEBSITE: www.hahnfamilywines.com
GPS COORDINATES: 36.390646, -121.365893

17 Manzoni Estate Vineyard

Work is a family affair at Manzoni Estate Vineyards. Brothers Michael and Mark, along with wives Gwen and Sabrina, respectfully, formed a partnership and opened their winery in 2004. The tasting room opened two years later.

The Manzoni family has been working this land since the 1930s, after the brothers' grandfather—Joseph Manzoni—emigrated to the U.S. from Switzerland in 1921. Back in the 1930s, this portion of the Salinas Valley was home to a very large Swiss population and many set up successful dairy operations. Joseph followed suit, but slowly turned his dairy business into farming. Joseph also was a winemaker, bringing with him the old-world traditions of making wine and Grappa, an Italian-based brandy. Joseph made the "refreshments" for family and friends, passing his knowledge down to his son Louie, and then to grandsons Michael and Mark.

The brothers' main reason for starting their winery was "to grow and make wine we can enjoy and share with our friends," according to Michael. In 1990, the family took 5.5 acres from their existing cash-crop land and planted Pinot Noir and Syrah. It wasn't until 1999 that they became serious about opening a winery. Now an established small boutique winery, Manzoni Estate Vineyard releases less than 2,000 case of wine annually. Their winemaker has been with them since the beginning—Steve Pessagno of Pessagno Winery (see page 54). It's interesting to point out that Steve's winery, also on River Road, was once a Swiss-run dairy, too.

> **WINE MYTH** "Only wealthy people can enjoy wine." — *Gwen Manzoni*

When we asked Michael what was the one thing a visitor should not miss when they come by, he responded: "The great views of our vineyard and our row-crop farming operation. We grow a variety of crops: lettuce, romaine, broccoli, carrots, spinach and seed beans. This is our main business."

The tasting room is small but darling. The long tasting bar is perched on three wine barrels with the flag of Switzerland prominently displayed behind the counter. Outside and around back, you'll find acres of Manzoni's vineyards and the aforementioned crops.

FEATURED WINE: Chardonnay, Pinot Noir, Syrah and Port
TASTING COST: $5 per person
HOURS: Saturday and Sunday, 11 AM-5 PM
LOCATION: 30981 River Road, Soledad
PHONE: 831-675-3398
WEBSITE: www.manzoniwines.com
GPS COORDINATES: 36.471365, -121.468223

Soledad

18 Paraiso Vineyards

When Richard Smith and Claudia Alexander met at the University of California at Davis in 1963, did they ever imagine that they would become the owners of one of Monterey County's most respected vineyards and wineries? Probably, yes.

The couple married in 1967 and following their dream, purchased their current property in   the Santa Lucia Highlands in 1973. Rich began planting their 400-acre property with wine grapes, selling the fruit to other ultra-premium producers. It wasn't until 1988 that the Smiths produced wines under the Paraiso name. Thirty-eight years later, Parasio hosts 3,000 acres of grapes spread throughout sixteen different vineyard blocks. What is most interesting about Paraiso is their deep commitment to sustainable growing; they are one of the first vineyards in the Santa Lucia Highlands to be SIP certified. Given by the Central Coast Vineyard Team, which Paraiso is a founding member, this "Sustainability in Practice" certification confirms that a winery has intituted certain protocols for being truly green.

WINE MYTH "Smaller crop = better quality." — *Dave Fleming*

Paraiso Vineyards—named after the moniker bestowed upon the nearby mountainside by early Spanish explorers—is a family-owned, sustainably farmed, 100-percent estate winery. Three generations of Smiths are involved in the family business, including Rich and Claudia's two adult children, Jason and Kacy, and their families. Jason is general manager of both the vineyard and winery, while Kacy is a track coach at the local high school. But Kacy stays involved with the winery; she's married to Dave Fleming, Paraiso's winemaker! Jason and his wife Jennifer Murphy-Smith—who oversees the tasting room—have three kids between them, and Kacy and Dave also have three, with the older ones working at the winery. Needless to say, when the Smith/Fleming brood gets together, that's one big party!

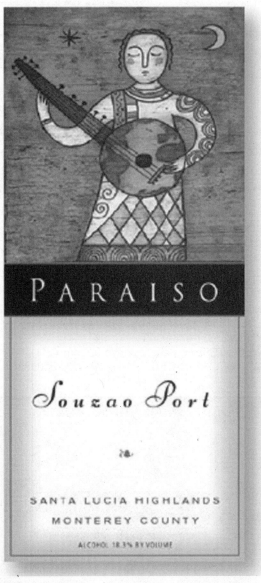

Farming for the future is a long-held philosophy for the Smith family. They have always been innovators—from research to practical hands-on knowledge—and have helped create a legacy of sustainable growing throughout the coast region. Besides helping to outline and establish the Santa Lucia Highlands AVA, they perfected many of the wine industry's standards, including advanced trellising and irrigation systems, mobile vineyard pressing and mechanical harvesting.

One reason for Paraiso's success can be attributed to winemaker Dave Fleming. With course work in enology from the University of

California at Davis, Dave became winemaker and production chief at Paraiso in 1999. Following a philosophy of letting the vineyards speak for themselves through minimal intervention, Dave said, "The wonderful Santa Lucia Highlands fruit I work with makes my job easy. I try not to get in the way of that special 'sense of place' being expressed in the bottle."

Paraiso Vineyard's tasting room opened in 1992. As you head inside, stop and take notice of the very large cork tree out front; it's fun to run your hands over the bark and imagine this is where cork comes from. Once inside, and with a glass of Paraiso's wine in hand, head out to the deck to take in the wonderful view of the Salinas River Valley. For shoppers, you'll love the stunning home décor and gift boutique, and for dog lovers, if you're lucky you might meet Paraiso's three winery dogs: Aero, a Golden Retriever; Irie, an Australian Shepherd; and Bleecker, a Goldendoodle.

FEATURED WINE: Pinot Noir, Chardonnay, Riesling and Syrah
TASTING COST: $5 (waived per bottle purchased)
HOURS: Monday-Thursday, 11 AM-4 PM; Friday-Sunday, 11 AM-5 PM
LOCATION: 38060 Paraiso Springs Road, Soledad
PHONE: 831-678-0300
WEBSITE: www.paraisovineyards.com
GPS COORDINATES: 36.378087, -121.340582

Soledad

19 Wrath

D riving to Wrath, we passed a curious-looking dilapidated house perched alongside the road within the winery's vineyards. Looking at each other quizzically, we just knew there had to be a story waiting for us, and Wrath's managing director Claire Marlin filled us in.

"The home once belonged to a Dr. Stafford," Claire said, explaining that the home—known as the "Stafford House"—was originally built in Salinas in 1890. "Due to neglect, the house was supposed to be torn down, but Dr. Mark Lemmon (the vineyard property's original owner) moved the house here in 1975 in hopes of turning it into offices and guest quarters." By the looks of the house, which easily can be seen on a vineyard knoll through Wrath's large tasting room windows, this was never done. Claire explained that Dr. Lemmon ran into a mountain of red tape when it came to the home's historical status and the permit process, so much so that he just gave up. But the story gets even better, and we'll come back to it toward the end of this listing.

Wrath originally was known as San Saba Vine-

Wrath's tasting room patio
(Photo courtesy of Wrath)

yards, one of the older vineyards in this region. Dr. Lemmon, a local plastic surgeon, purchased the 70-acre property and planted it with grapevines himself in the 1970s. He loved wine, being first exposed to it by his father, a prominent architect in Dallas. Together, the two made regular trips to Europe and during these forays, the younger Lemmon learned to appreciate wine, especially during excursions into

the Burgundy region of France.

Over the years that followed, Dr. Lemmon successfully ran both his medical practice and the vineyard. His second wife—Barbara Thomas Lemmon—had a son by the name of Michael Thomas. In 2007, Dr. Lemmon was well into his 80s and being unable to keep up with the demands of being both vineyard and winery owner, he sold the business to Michael.

Born in Texas, Michael graduated from Duke University and received a Ph.D. in classical art and archaeology from the University of Texas at Austin. Here he eventually obtained a research position after teaching at many other universities. Over the last 16 years, he has been leading two excavations in Italy, at a Roman site near Pompeii and at an Etruscan site northeast of Florence. Thus, the reason Claire Marlin was helping us. "Michael has an amazing palette in his own right," she said. "With his work, he gets to taste wine all over the world."

Wanting to bring San Saba Vineyards into the 21st century, Michael rebranded the winery with the name "Wrath" in 2008, a periodic reflection of the soil and weather of the region. And even though he is sometimes a half a world away, Michael is committed to the winery and oversees both the winemaking and vineyard practices, including Wrath's aggressive vineyard rejuvenation program of replanting large sections of the estate San Saba Vineyard with Pinot Noir, Chardonnay and Syrah.

Wrath's winemaker is Sabrine Rodems. Earning a degree from the University of California in Los Angeles in theatre, film and television in 1992, Sabrine worked several years with the San Francisco Opera and the film industry, as well. But she always harbored a love for science, coupled with a passion for food and wine. Following her dream, Sabrine obtained her master's degree in enology from the University of California at Davis. "She joined Wrath in 2004 and brings a nice sense of balance and elegance to our team," Claire said.

Wrath's tasting room may surprise you, as the color theme is black and white and the mood is stark yet elegant. At the far end of the room stands a stately fireplace and a long wooden table dressed in fine dishware as if awaiting the arrival of a party. Wrath has a very successful food- and wine-pairing program, the creation of Chef Brian Overhauser. For more information, please visit Wrath's website.

Now for that teaser regarding the Stafford House: The Queen Anne cottage has become such an icon in the area that Michael smartly included the dwelling on every Wrath label. If you look closely at the bottom of their labels, you'll see the famous silhouette. Even though the house has never been restored to its original state, it regally shares an intimate legacy with the wonderful wines of Wrath.

FEATURED WINE: Sauvignon Blanc, Chardonnay, Pinot Noir and Syrah
TASTING COST: $10 and up depending on tasting experience choice
HOURS: Thursday through Monday, 11 AM-5 PM
LOCATION: 35801 Foothill Road, Soledad
PHONE: 831-678-2212
WEBSITE: www.wrathwines.com
GPS COORDINATES: 36.4079, -121.386352

More Area Wineries

Carmel

Taste Morgan
LOCATION: 204 Crossroads Blvd., Carmel
PHONE: 831-626-3700
WEBSITE: www.morganwinery.com

Carmel-by-the-Sea

Otter Cove Wines
LOCATION: Carmel Plaza/Ocean Avenue, Carmel-by-the-Sea
PHONE: 831-320-3050
WEBSITE: www.ottercovewines.com

Tudor Wines
LOCATION: Carmel Plaza/Ocean Avenue, Carmel-by-the-Sea
PHONE: 831-224-2116
WEBSITE: www.tudorwines.com

Carmel Valley

Boekennogen Vineyards & Winery
LOCATION: 24 W. Carmel Valley Road, Carmel Valley
PHONE: 831-659-4215
WEBSITE: www.boekenoogenwines.com

Chateau Sinnet Winery
LOCATION: 13746 Center Street, Carmel Valley
PHONE: 831-659-2244
WEBSITE: www.chateausinnet.com

Georis Winery
LOCATION: 4 Pilot Road, Carmel Valley
PHONE: 831-659-1050
WEBSITE: www.georiswine.com

Monterey
Baywood Cellars
LOCATION: 381 Cannery Row, Monterey
PHONE: 831-645-9035
WEBSITE: www.baywood-cellars.com

Salinas
Marilyn Remark Wines
LOCATION: 645 River Road, Salinas
PHONE: 831-455-9310
WEBSITE: www.remarkwines.com

Winery Notes

Winery Notes

Side Trips

Big Sur Coast

The coastal drive from Monterey south on Highway 1 is beyond breathtaking—nearly every turn on this narrow, twisting ribbon of asphalt reveals spectacular cliffs, coves and more.

The 90-mile stretch of land beginning in Carmel and heading south is referred to as the Big Sur Coast. While parts of the Big Sur Coast are private property, much is open to the public, including several state parks and the Los Padres National Forest.

Point Lobos State Reserve has been described as the world's most dramatic meeting of land and sea. Just a few miles south of Carmel, this jewel of a state reserve features trails, tide pools and sea lions (www. parks.ca.gov).

During winter, whale watching is a popular activity from the highway's numerous cliffside pull-outs. One of the most popular places to see whales is Point Sur State Historic Park's lightstation. Perched atop a spectacular 361-foot high volcanic promontory, this historic lightstation has been in continuous operation since 1889 and is now staffed by volunteers (limited reservations available: 831-625-4419).

Another popular destination is Pfeiffer Big Sur State Park, about an hour's drive south from Carmel. The park's lodge and campgrounds are situated in the picturesque coastal mountains and redwood forests along the Big Sur River (www.parks.ca.gov).

Historic Monterey

The Spanish first landed here in 1602, but it wasn't until 1769 that Captain Gaspar de Portolà and Father Junipero Serra arrived together and established the Presidio of Monterey and Mission de San Carlos Borromeo de Monterey, Spain's second mission in Alta California. Changes came—the mission was soon moved to Carmel, Spain's Alta California in 1821 became part of Mexico, and finally in 1846, Monterey was captured and claimed by the United States.

Monterey is a bustling coastal tourist city, yet it retains much of its celebrated flavor, especially with its historic adobes. Due to the lack

The Monterey Custom House is California's Historic Landmark #1.

of easily accessible forests, adobe brick (dried blocks of mud and straw) was the most common building material, even among the growing city's richest and most prominent citizens. Today many of those early adobe homes remain as part of Monterey State Historic Park (www. parks.ca.gov), often with original furnishings from their early owners. You can even visit the historic Stevenson House named for famed Scottish author Robert Louis Stevenson. In late 1879, while recovering from one of his many illnesses, he resided in what was then known as the French Hotel.

Three of Monterey's many historic adobe buildings should not to be missed: First is the Custom House, California's Historic Landmark #1, located next to Fisherman's Wharf. The Custom House is where taxes were collected from trading ships during the Spanish, Mexican and early American periods. The second adobe is the Pacific House in the nearby Custom House Plaza; it serves as a museum and interpretive center and provides a look at Monterey's colorful history. Third is the City of Monterey's Colton Hall, California's first official U.S. government building. Here in 1849 California's Constitution was created and ratified by representatives concerned about voting rights, whether California would be a free state or a slave state and where boundaries would be located. Because eight delegates didn't speak English, California's Constitution was written in both English and Spanish.

Carmel Mission

California's original Spanish missions have become important historical landmarks, something that nearly every fourth grader in the Golden State learns about in school. The mission at Carmel was the second of the 21 missions established between 1769 and 1823. Today it is a favorite destination for visitors from around the world. This is where the founder Father Serra died in 1784 and was buried. A controversy in 1882 caused his casket to be disinterred to confirm that Serra was indeed the occupant. He was, and Serra was reburied near his longtime friend Father Crespi. Serra's original casket was put on display at the mission.

The church underwent a restoration in 1931 and much of that restoration work is documented in the Harry Downie Museum located near the main church. Several of the mission's rooms have been restored and there are hundreds of artifacts to view. There is even a reconstruction of what was California's first library, which was established right here. The church and mission grounds are so picturesque that it's not unusual to find local artists stationed about the grounds drawing and painting pictures of the church and the beautiful flowers that are everywhere. There is a small mission gift shop at the entrance where entry fees are collected (www.carmelmission.org).

Cannery Row & Monterey Bay Aquarium

A trip to Monterey, more times than not, includes the city's famed Cannery Row. With several wine tasting rooms located within a couple of blocks along this notable road, be sure to take the time to wander and discover the unique delights of this historic sardine cannery empire.

This area became famous because of John Steinbeck's book by the same name, but it didn't immediately become a tourist attraction. That didn't occur until well after the mid-1950s, following the collapse of

the entire Monterey Bay sardine fishery due to overfishing. Today, the old sardine processing plants have been transformed into restaurants, gift shops, art galleries and wine-tasting venues (www.canneryrow. com).

At one end of Cannery Row, San Carlos Beach is a popular scuba diving access point and kayak launching area. Through the middle of all this winds a popular paved pedestrian and bike trail; it starts in nearby Pacific Grove and meanders for 18 miles—much of it along the coast—past the Monterey Bay Aquarium, Monterey's historic Custom

House and Fisherman's Wharf, Seaside, Fort Ord, and Marina, finally ending in Castroville, the artichoke capital of the world. If you don't have your own bike or kayak, there are several businesses where you can rent them for an hour, a day, or more.

A must-stop is the world-renown Monterey Bay Aquarium. With nearly 200 galleries and exhibits dedicated to the many habitats of Monterey Bay, fan favorites include the Kelp Forest, Sea Otter exhibit and one of the largest jellyfish galleries in the world (831-648-4800 or www.montereybayaquarium.org).

National Steinbeck Center

Most of us have read one or more of John Steinbeck's great novels including *East of Eden, Cannery Row, Of Mice and Men, Tortilla Flat* and his 1940 Pulitzer Prize-winning *The Grapes of Wrath*. Steinbeck, who was born in the small town of Salinas in 1902, used this area as the backdrop for some of his novels about the plight of farm workers, a picture that didn't always paint the land-owning farmers in the best of light. For this reason, he was not always welcome here.

John Steinbeck's truck and camper from his 1960 cross-country trip.

But times have changed. Today, Salinas honors their great native son and author with the National Steinbeck Center (831-775-4721 or www.steinbeck.org). At the center, you have an opportunity to follow the man's life and career; exhibits range from original manuscripts to numerous clips from the many films made from his novels, including *Life Boat*, which was directed by Alfred Hitchcock. One of the more interesting exhibits is Steinbeck's green GMC pickup and camper that he drove around the country in 1960 at the age of 61, gathering stories for what would become his 1962 book *Travels with Charley in Search of America*. Charley was his wife's poodle.

Monterey County Agricultural Museum

As you drive south along U.S. 101 in search of wine, you'll soon leave the fields of lettuce, strawberries and artichokes and encounter thousands of acres of the vineyards. This is the perfect place to experience firsthand the region's rich agricultural history at the Monterey County Agricultural Museum in King City (831-385-8020 or www. mcarim.org).

Located within San Lorenzo County Park, the indoor museum is situated in an oversized barn; here you will learn about farming history and farming practices in Monterey County. Outside the main museum exhibit building, farm equipment manufactured and used from the late 1800s to pieces leftover from the WWII-era can be seen. There's a 1927 Farmall Regular, described as the first "all-purpose" tractor, along with bean planters, hay rakes and side-hill combines.

Several more buildings dot the museum grounds. An old house once owned by long-time local company Spreckels Sugar was moved here. The company used the 24-foot by 26-foot house as housing for local farm workers. You will also find a blacksmith shop, La Gloria School (circa 1880) and even a 1903 train depot.

Mission San Antonio de Padua

Mission San Antonio de Padua, located outside of the town of Jolon in southern Monterey County, is one of California's more interesting missions, especially if you are a wine lover. Here you will find an original Mission grapevine, planted in the 1780s.

Located on the grounds of Fort Hunter Liggett—an active military base and the nation's largest U.S. Army Reserve command post—California's third mission was built in 1771. One of the exhibit rooms features the mission's wine cellar, processing and storage area, a testament to the importance of wine to the early Jesuit padres. The outside grounds include the remains of a very elaborate canal system for irrigating crops—including wine grapes—as well as the remnants of a millrace, cemetery and the ruins of the majordomo's home.

To enter Fort Hunter Liggett, you must have in your possession, and show to Army personnel, your vehicle registration, proof of registration and insurance and a valid ID for every adult—no exceptions. It is strongly advised you call ahead to confirm the military base is open to public access, and confirm the mission is open (831-385-4478 or www.missionsanantonio.net).

Garland Ranch Regional Park

Found on W. Carmel Valley Road, this 4,462-acre park is popular for its many hiking, horseback, mountain biking and birding trails. Here you will find Garzas Creek, the Carmel River, a redwood canyon, waterfall and historic buildings. The park is also dog friendly, offering many off-leash areas, hiking trails and specially-designed water fountains for both hikers and canines. Be sure to check in with the visitor center for trail and birding maps and rules regarding dogs (www.seemonterey.com/garland-ranch-regional-park-carmel-valley-california).

For More Information

Monterey County Vintners and Growers Association
PO Box 1793
Monterey, CA 93942
831-375-9400
www.montereywines.org

Monterey County Convention and Visitors Bureau
PO Box 1770
Monterey, CA 93942
888-221-1010
www.seemonterey.com

Carmel-by-the-Sea Chamber of Commerce
PO Box 4444
Carmel, CA 93921
831-550-4333
www.carmelcalifornia.org

Salinas Valley Chamber of Commerce
119 E. Alisal Street
Salinas, CA 93901
831-751-7725
www.salinaschamber.com

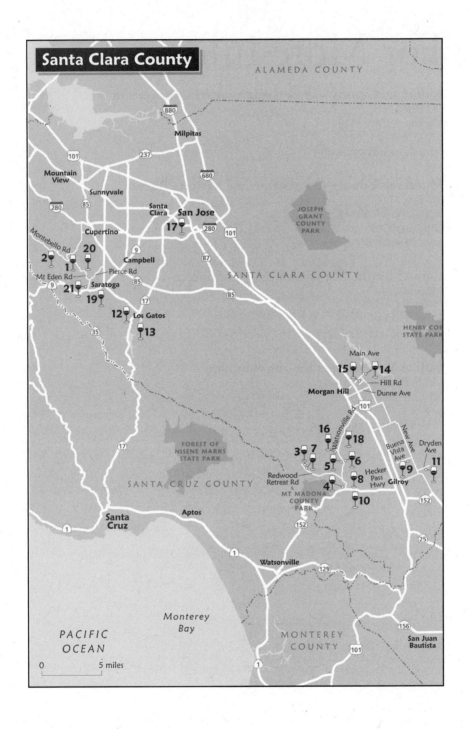

Santa Clara County

Chapter Two

Santa Clara County is more closely associated with microchips and the Silicon Valley than it is with wine. After all, it is home to Apple, Sun Microsystems, Hewlett Packard, Google, Yahoo, eBay and Intel. Yet in spite of the county's overwhelming urbanization, some of California's best wineries are found here, with one of the biggest—J. Lohr— located in the city of San Jose. While expansive development and population growth has taken its toll on agricultural land that could be growing excellent vineyards, there remains plenty of open space, especially in the southern end of the Santa Clara Valley.

Within the Central Coast AVA (American Viticultural Area),

View from the Santa Cruz Mountains looking toward the Santa Clara Valley.

the county's Santa Clara Valley AVA is part of the larger San Francisco Bay AVA and includes two smaller AVAs, Pacheco Pass and San Ysidro. Each AVA offers different soil, terrain and weather conditions that contribute to the unique complexity of the varietals grown within their boundaries. Along much of the county's western border, the Santa Cruz Mountains act as a natural barrier to the Pacific Ocean's cooling influence on the hot interior valleys. There are exceptions, with Hecker Pass and Pajaro Pass funneling cool coastal breezes through the mountains and into localized areas of the inland valleys.

Decades prior to the creation of Silicon Valley, pioneer winemakers had discovered the region's capacity for growing excellent wine grapes. The Spanish missionaries were first, with a few European immigrants following in their footsteps. Charles LeFranc arrived here from France in 1852 and began planting French grapes rather than the Mission grapes that the Spanish missions had introduced in the 18th century. This marked the beginning of Almaden Vineyards. In 1892, Paul Masson, another French winemaker, settled here and introduced sparkling wines, which he called "champagne." In 1905, Masson built his chateau on a bluff overlooking the Santa Clara Valley. Now known as The Mountain Winery, it is included on the National Register of Historic Places. It's also a great place to enjoy plays, major concerts and other entertainment in their expansive outdoor amphitheater.

Speaking of entertainment, if you have time, there are many fun things to add to your wine-tasting itinerary. San Jose's Rosicrucian Egyptian Museum will take you back in history several thousand years with the largest collection of Egyptian artifacts in western North America. More recent history is told at the Intel Museum where its historic artifacts include early semiconductor-chip technology. For California mission buffs, Mission Santa Clara de Asis, founded in 1777 as the eighth of California's 21 Spanish missions, is located on the grounds of Santa Clara University. For thrill seekers, California's Great America features the most water rides and kids' rides in Northern California. If a quiet hike is more your style, then head over to Picchetti Ranch where you will find several miles of trails through the woodland hills, all part of Midpeninsula Regional Open Space District.

Cupertino

1 Picchetti Winery

Leslie Pantling, owner of Picchetti Winery, wants you to save yourself the trip to the Napa Valley and come visit her place instead! Located southwest of Cupertino on Montebello Road, Leslie would be honored to have you spend the day at her historic winery, tasting her award-winning wine and relaxing in the beautiful picnic area. Afterward, explore the many hiking trails of the adjacent Picchetti Ranch Open Space Reserve.

Leslie has owned the historic winery since 1998. The Picchetti family gave her the rights to the historic winery's name, and she leases the land and buildings from the Midpeninsula Regional Open Space District (MROSD). MROSD preserves thousands of acres of bay land, foothill and mountainous open space in their 26 preserves.

Picchetti Winery history goes back to the 1880s when Italian

immigrants Vincenso and Secondo Picchetti purchased 160 acres and planted Zinfandel, Carignane and Petite Sirah. They sold their fruit to other wineries up until 1896, when they decided to create their own label. They established Picchetti Winery and built the two-story brick winery the same year, which today serves as Picchetti's tasting room.

In 1904, Vicenso passed away and left the winery and its now 500 acres to his sons Antone and John. Prohibition in 1919 forced the

brothers to sell acreage and convert some of the vineyard to orchards. They also expanded their livestock. A fun side note is that John was a birder; he built aviaries and bred several species of birds, one being the peacock. Today, direct descendents of John's peacocks still roam the grounds. During the 1960s, the ranch became unprofitable and the family had to make hard decisions. They ceased commercial wine production in 1963 and in 1977, sold the remaining land to the MROSD.

Before becoming a winery owner, Leslie was part of Silicon Valley's high-tech life, although she had also been a grower for nearby Ridge Vineyards for many years. When the opportunity presented itself to purchase what had become Sunrise Winery and change the name back to the original Picchetti, Leslie didn't hesitate. She took over the lease for the buildings and land and immediately brought in new production equipment and a top-notch crew and tasting-room staff. Today, Picchetti Winery produces upwards of 9,000 cases of wine annually, using estate grapes from their 3.5 acres of Chardonnay, Cabernet Sauvignon and 110-year-old Zinfandel vines. They also source additional grapes when needed.

Picchetti's winemaker is Aimee Baker, a rarity because female winemakers are, unfortunately, uncommon in the Santa Cruz Mountains. "Aimee's focus is to let each of the vineyards show its potential in the glass," Leslie explained. "Aimee strongly believes that great wine is grown in the vineyard and she is inspired by the quality of fruit she gets to work with." Schooled at the University of California at Davis where she obtained her master's degree in enology and viticulture, Aimee's prior career was that of a collegiate rowing coach.

We loved Picchetti Winery's historic grounds and tasting room. The winery complex, which is on the National Register of Historic Places, is dotted with interesting artifacts and interpretive panels that tell more about the site. Inside the very large tasting room, you'll find a tasting counter just about as long as the room itself, antler chandeliers, plank floors and original brick walls. If you stand facing the tasting bar and look at the far right corner of the back wall, directly above the huge wooden wine tank from the 1915 World's Fair, you'll see sagging bricks, a result of the 1906 San Francisco earthquake.

Because Picchetti Winery is a private business operating under a cooperative lease with MROSD, they have to abide by strict rules regarding their picnic area. If you're planning a picnic, we strongly urge you to visit their website for more information. Also note that pets are not allowed anywhere on the grounds, with the exception of registered service animals.

Picchetti maintains a second tasting room in South Lake Tahoe that features the same tasting list (3135 Harrison Avenue, 530-541-1500).

FEATURED WINES: Cabernet Sauvignon, Chardonnay, Zinfandel and Sangiovese
TASTING COST: $5, refunded with purchase
HOURS: Daily, 11 AM-5 PM
LOCATION: 13100 Montebello Road, Cupertino
PHONE: 408-741-1310
WEBSITE: www.picchetti.com
GPS COORDINATES: 37.295799, -122.087767

2 Ridge Vineyards

J uly in California can be a bear. Such was the case when we visited Ridge Vineyards in northeastern Santa Cruz Mountains the day before the 4th of July. We arrived around 9:30 AM and were greeted in the already warm sunshine by Ridge tasting room manager and entertaining wine blogger Christopher Watkins (www.blog.ridgewine.com). Christopher showed us into the large tasting room, and a few minutes later, Ridge CEO and winemaking legend Paul Draper arrived, along with his dog Bodhi (pronounced Bodie). A Samoyed, Bodhi joined Paul as he took us on an exclusive private tour of the inner-workings of Ridge Vineyards.

Quick history: In 1885, Dr. Osea Perrone purchased 180 acres on a 2500 feet elevation ridge where the winery is now located. He terraced the steep slopes, and the following year planted Cabernet vineyards. He then built Monte Bello Winery, using native redwood and limestone, and released his first vintage in 1892. The winery continued

producing wines up to Prohibition in 1919 then resumed limited production when Prohibition was lifted in 1933, but by the early '40s, the remaining vineyards were abandoned.

In the 1940s, William Short purchased an adjacent winery property and its abandoned vineyard and replanted several sections with Cabernet Sauvignon. In 1954 Short sold his business to Dave Bennion and three partners, all Stanford Research Institute engineers who happened to love wine. They made a half-barrel's worth of Cabernet that turned out to be surprisingly good, and thus the partners' hobby turned into a much bigger enterprise, so much so that they re-bonded the winery in 1962. Over the next ten years, the foursome increased the vineyard from 15 to 45 acres and by 1968 the winery annually produced 3,000 cases.

In 1969, Paul Draper joined the partnership. Under his careful guidance, Draper helped restore the old Perrone winery, which the partners had purchased in 1968, along with the Monte Bello vineyards. Now more than 40 years later, Ridge Vineyards encompasses 125 planted acres and produces 80,000 cases of wine annually. Paul is CEO and head winemaker of Ridge Vineyards, and the driving force behind the winery's great domestic and international success.

We followed Paul and Bodhi by car farther up the ridge to the 125-year-old production winery and spent an hour in one of Ridge's expansive and refreshingly cool barrel rooms. Paul's stellar reputation

> **WINE MYTH** "You should drink what the wine critics tell you to drink rather than what tastes good to you. (No one tells you how you like your eggs cooked or your steak cooked)." — *Paul Draper*

as a winemaker for more than five decades has made him a household name within all facets of the wine industry. For example, two major achievements occurred during both the 1976 Judgment of Paris wine tasting competition and again in 2006 during the 30th anniversary of that event. Both competitions pitted French wines against California wines, and even though Ridge placed fifth out of ten in the 1976 event with its 1971 Monte Bello Cabernet—from Paul's third vintage at Ridge—the same wine, same vintage, won the 2006 event by 18 points. All this aside, Paul—a modest, gentle-natured man who looks much younger than his 75 years—made it a point to mention he has delegated the day-to-day winemaking duties at the Monte Bello winery to Ridge vice president and winemaker Eric Baugher, though the two taste and make the winemaking decisions together.

While in the barrel room, Paul asked if we wanted to try some 2009 Monte Bello Cabernet from the barrel. How could one turn down such a wonderful offer? With glasses in hand, Paul used a wine thief and drew us each a taste. Considering the wine had been in the barrel for only six months, it was amazingly elegant on the palette and had a strikingly smooth finish for being so young. Paul then entertained us with a great story about the 2009 harvest, which you can read in our full in-depth interview with him at **www.WineWherever.com**.

Leaving the Monte Bello barrel room, we went down two and three levels and into the historic cellar, which is still used today for barrel aging just as it was more than 125 years ago (a photo of the cellar is featured on the cover of this book). When we inquired about the impact of the San Francisco earthquake of 1906 and also the Loma Prieta earthquake in 1989, Paul said that the building was built into limestone bedrock, so damage during both major quakes was minimal. "Our appellation—Santa Cruz Mountains—is cut in two by the San Andreas Fault," said Paul, noting that Ridge sits on the North American Plate portion of the wine appellation.

Paul heading down to Ridge's historic wine cellar, which is featured on the cover.

For those not familiar with California geology, the North American Plate and the Pacific Plate makes up the famed fault, and the plates move horizontally against each other, not up and down. "The

Pacific Plate is going north and it's dragging us with it, and friction is holding us with the Pacific Plate as it moves north. The fault is just a half mile west of us—and 2700 feet below us."

The end of our interview found us back in Ridge's tasting room, where Christopher uncorked some exquisite Monte Bello selections from the 1990s. The four of us shared these wonderful offerings, including wine from Ridge's other winery in Sonoma County—Lytton Springs where John Olney is vice president of winemaking.

Before we left, we asked why the winery no longer was called Monte Bello Winery, its original namesake. We learned that the coveted name had been sold to a third party in the 1940s and when the partners tried to use the name, they ran into legal problems. "Monte Bello Ridge" was the alternative, but that name came with the same issues. Finally, "Ridge" worked, and eventually the partners were able to secure the trademarked name "Monte Bello."

The trip up the mountain to Ridge Vineyards is beautiful and nearly every turn of Monte Bello Road brings a surprise. In the warm months, the biggest surprise is cyclists; with an elevation change of 2000 feet, this road is a haven for hard-core road cyclists, so stay alert. As you near the top of the ridge, be sure to look east: on a clear day, the view is breathtaking.

Ridge Vineyards offers a shaded picnic area, but tables fill up fast. If you walk up the pathway above the picnic area to take in more amazing views of San Francisco and the Bay Area, heed the "beware of rattlesnakes" signs at least in summer; apparently snakes enjoy the view, too. And last, no pets are allowed in the picnic area, on the grounds or in the tasting room whatsoever, and staff is very firm in enforcing this rule. Of course clearly-identified service animals are allowed.

Ridge offers many tasting opportunities to excite any wine lover. Because their offerings change periodically, check their website for the most current information.

FEATURED WINES: Cabernet Sauvignon, Zinfandel and Chardonnay
TASTING COST: $5-20
HOURS: Saturday and Sunday, 11 AM-4 PM
LOCATION: 17100 Monte Bello Road, Cupertino
PHONE: 408-867-3233
WEBSITE: www.ridgewine.com
GPS COORDINATES: 37.300278, -122.117349

3 Fernwood Cellars

Fernwood Cellars owner Matt Oetinger is the fifth generation to work this piece of land. His great-great-great grandparents Charles and Annis Sanders homesteaded here in the 1860s, coming to California from their native Nova Scotia. In 1891, Charles built a 20-room Victorian hotel and called it "Redwood Retreat." The lavish grounds included lawn tennis courts and the second outdoor swimming pool ever built in California. The family planted table grapes, along with a garden and orchards.

In 1908, the hotel burned to the ground, but Charles replaced it with a lodge-style building and added cabins along the nearby creek. Beginning in 1910, the couple's youngest child Annis "Gypsy" Sanders

Redwood Retreat 1890

(Photo courtesy of Fernwood Cellars)

operated the resort until the Depression forced her to close in 1929. In the 1930s, Gypsy's son Charles Pond married Elsie Malek and they vacationed on the property. In the 1960s, fire struck again when partying trespassers torched many of the aging cabins.

In 1991, Linda Pond-Oetinger (the daughter of Charles and Elsie Pond), along with her mother Elsie, then a widow, built a home at Redwood Retreat. Linda restored many of the buildings, including the original Sanders home. Linda and her son Matt—the fifth generation—also planted wine grapes on their historical property.

Matt's father Lew Oetinger, divorced from Matt's mother, lived in the Sierra foothills and planted a vineyard himself. It was at his father's vineyard where Matt was first exposed to the business aspects of winemaking, while working toward a degree in biology at the University of California at Davis. Upon graduation in 1995, Matt had the honor of working directly for Dr. Jim Wolpert, the chair of the university's famed viticulture and enology department. Finally, after employment at other wineries, including Clos LaChance (see page 135), Matt established Fernwood Cellars in 1999.

Besides overseeing his family's own vineyards and production facility, Matt manages 20 additional vineyards, two of which are the

Bates Ranch's Vineyard and Vanumanutagi Vineyard. Bates Ranch, located in the southern-most end of the Santa Cruz Mountains, was once the home of John Bates, a friend of Robert F. Kennedy. The story goes that Kennedy was at the ranch the weekend Marilyn Monroe died. Conspiracy theorists beg to differ.

Fannie Stevenson, the widow of Robert Louis Stevenson (he died in Samoa in 1894), once owned the land where the Vanumanutagi Vineyard now stands. She named the property "Vanumanutagi," which in Samoan means "valley of the singing birds," and lived there periodically from 1900 until her passing in 1914. The property, which is adjacent to Fernwood Cellars, stayed in the Stevenson family until 1969, when Leo Ware purchased it and, honoring Stevenson, retained the property name. Eleven years later, Ware planted nine acres of grapes, naming each block after a Stevenson novel, with another 6.5 acres planted in 2006, according to Matt.

Regarding their tasting room, Matt and his wife Tiffany are working toward a retreat-like atmosphere for visitors—inside and especially outside—just like the old days. The couple has two children and only time will tell if this sixth generation will create its own legacies at Fernwood Cellars.

Finding Fernwood Cellars is challenging if you're unfamiliar with the area. When heading northwest on Redwood Retreat Road, upon reaching the Y-intersection with Mt. Madonna Road, be sure to bear right. The winery is about four miles from the intersection.

FEATURED WINE: Cabernet Sauvignon, Chardonnay, Syrah and Zinfandel
TASTING COST: $10, can be applied toward purchase
HOURS: Third weekend of the month, 12 PM-5 PM
LOCATION: 7137 Redwood Retreat Road, Gilroy
PHONE: 408-848-0611
WEBSITE: www.fernwoodcellars.com
GPS COORDINATES: 37.042223, -121.716957

4 | Hecker Pass Winery

At Hecker Pass Winery, winemaking is a family tradition dating back 150 years. Patriarch Mario Fortino is Hecker Pass Winery's "winemaster," a term affectionately used by his son Carlo Fortino. Carlo told us that his father is a third generation winemaker from Italy and that his love for old-world winemaking traditions stems from his being born and raised in the Calabria region of Italy (also known as the "toe of Italy"), in the town of Cozenza to be exact. It was here that Mario's great grandfather started making wine back in the mid-1880s and, in later years, taught Mario the craft.

Wanting a better future and more opportunities, Mario immigrated to the United States in 1959. Only 21 years old, the young immigrant learned to speak English quickly while working for wineries in the region he now calls home. But knowing Mario, he more than likely taught his employers a thing or two about winemaking! "We had a very

small winery in Italy," Mario said, citing that over the years, he has learned much. "I have learned that hard work, dedication and family are what are important to having a successful and fulfilling life. I am very proud and happy that our family tradition will be carried on by my son and grandchildren," he said, in an Italian accent that would make any woman with a romantic heart swoon. Besides son Carlo—who is the assistant winemaker, marketing director and oversees the daily operation of their very busy family winery—Mario's granddaughter Jennifer is the winery's event coordinator and Michael, his grandson, is their vineyard manager. (To learn more about Mario and Carlo, read their interview at **www.WineWherever.com**.)

Hecker Pass Winery is located at the foot of Mt. Madonna on the Hecker Pass Highway. When we pulled in, it was a weekday and the winery wasn't busy. We actually caught Carlo and Mario laying a brick walkway. The two had some inkling we would be in the area that week, but didn't know when. Mario quickly greeted us as Carlo went to change. Once we were all together, we had a fabulous time learning about their nearly 40-year-old winery and going on a tour of the winery and barrel room, which housed giant wooden wine casks. But to our surprise, just around the corner from the tasting room was a breathtaking, full turn-key event facility. Called the "La Vigna Event

Center," the indoor 1,000-square-foot grand salon was built entirely by father and son, and the expansive 5,500-square-foot outdoor covered area was complemented by the beautiful vineyard setting. "We host many events and weddings," said Carlo, who proceeded to show us the rest of the facility, including a luxurious bridal dressing room and full outside bar set-up.

Needless to say, devotion to tradition and hospitality reigns supreme at Hecker Pass Winery. We felt like we had become part of their large, extended Italian family, laughing and trading stories. When we

> **WINE MYTH** "White Zinfandel is made from white grapes." — *Carlo Fortino*

left, Carlo gave us a bottle of their Carignane as a thank you gift, but it was father Mario who absolutely insisted we also take a bottle of his Chianti. Ken grinned, as he recalled drinking Chianti when he was in Vietnam during the war; he asked Mario how come his wine, in a slender bottle, didn't look like the stereotypical, basket-wrapped bottle of Chianti? Mario just laughed an all-knowing laugh and saw us off to our next winery.

When we returned home from our research trip, we shared our wine with neighbors (which we do often), and one neighbor, who is very particular about what wine he drinks, ended up ordering several cases of the Chianti! The last time we saw Mario, he was thrilled that the Chianti was such a hit, and was even more tickled to learn that his new fan was Italian, just like him.

All the wines at Hecker Pass are estate grown. Their unique Italian varietals are dry farmed, head pruned (no trellis), hand picked and hand processed. The family utilizes sustainable growth practices, and the results are evident in their wonderful fruit-forward wines, including semi-sweet and dessert wines such as Muscat, Cream Sherry, Marsala and Ruby Port.

FEATURED WINE: Petite Sirah, Zinfandel, Carignane and Grenache
TASTING COST: Complimentary
HOURS: Daily, 10 AM-5 PM
LOCATION: 4605 Hecker Pass Hwy., Gilroy
PHONE: 408-842-8755
WEBSITE: www.heckerpasswinery.com
GPS COORDINATES: 37.0134, -121.65439

5 Jason-Stephens Winery

Most wine lovers can agree that great wines begin on the vine, and the owners of Jason-Stephens Winery are in total agreement. Here you will find an amazing working relationship between a young winemaker and a seasoned grape grower—Jason Goelz and Stephen "Steve" Dorcich, respectively.

Bowing to wisdom and age first, Steve Dorcich, in his fifty-somethings, has been farming nearly all his life. Starting at the age of eight, Steve worked on his family's farm, located in what is now the Silicon Valley. By twelve, he was driving a tractor and maintaining their pear and peach orchards. But speed was his interest, something that wasn't going to happen on the back of a tractor; once grown, Steve became an open-wheeled Formula 2 racer. Later, Steve and a buddy formed an

offshore boat racing team and in 1990 placed first in a world champi-
onship. But over the years, boats became faster than the twin 1,400 hp
engines he was using; it was then Steve gravitated back to life on his
3-mile per hour tractor. He purchased land in Santa Clara's Uvas Valley
and in 1989 began to plant his vineyard.

The younger man in this story—Jason Goelz—has quite the list
of accomplishments to his credit, too. In his early 20s, Jason already
knew he wanted to make wine a part of his life. Leaving a corporate
job, he became a wine distributor and learned that side of the trade. In
1999, he attended California Polytechnic State University in San Luis
Obispo and earned the college's very first minor degree in wine and
viticulture (but majored in finance and accounting with an additional
minor in economics). At this point, Jason was only 23.

> **WINE MYTH** "Wine 'legs' or 'tears' indicate high quality." — *Jason Goelz*

Jason met Steve when he purchased grapes from him for his home
winemaking endeavors. Recognizing the high quality of Steve's fruit,
and the fact that the elder grape grower believed strongly in sustainable
agriculture, Jason suggested a winery partnership. Steve agreed. The
business was formed, a name for the winery was chosen (a combination
of both partners' names) and in April 2007, Jason-Stephens Winery
became a reality.

This hands-on partnership between winemaker and grape grower, who are in close proximity to each other since Jason's winery and
tasting room sit adjacent to the north block of Dorcich Vineyards, is
definitely working. "The vineyard manager knows exactly what to do
in the field to make the grapes perfect at harvest, based on the desires
of the winemaker," Jason shared. "After harvest, the winemaker's role is
to care for the grapes as they mature into superb wines. Just as a parent
guides a child into adulthood, the winemaker brings these handcrafted
wines to life." And the duo has done just that—creating great wines
that are a testament to their combined philosophies.

In hearing Jason's story, you have to give him kudos for following
his dream, especially at his age. And his approach when it comes to creating the perfect wine—and that all-so-important brand and customer
base—is admirable. "We don't look for customers; we want to build
friends, family and life-long loyal wine lovers," Jason explained. "We

are all individuals in search of meaning in our daily lives—meaning in what we eat, what we drink and what we wear. As a winemaker, my goal is to change people's lives for the better because of what I've created. Without our discerning fans who enjoy our fine wines, Jason-Stephens would be nothing more than another California winery." Well put.

The winery's tasting room is radiant and engaging. Inside, you'll find hardwood floors, large windows behind the bar that look out over the winery's production facility and a unique concrete tasting bar top featuring embedded, lighted winery logos. Outside is a large seating area prepped and ready for guests during the fair weather months. Dakota—a Golden Retriever—is the winery's official "winery dog." Jason said his dog is his best marketing tool. "Dakota is the sweetest dog. As our hospitality manager, he greets people, but protects the winery as a security guard, too," Jason said, noting that Dakota is good at keeping deer out of the vineyard. "And he licks up spilt wine so not a drop is wasted!"

The entry to Jason-Stephens Winery is easy to spot: watch for towering palm trees that line the driveway on both sides. At the end of the drive, the tasting room will be to your right.

FEATURED WINE: Cabernet Sauvignon, Zinfandel, Syrah and Chardonnay
TASTING COST: $5
HOURS: Summer, 12 PM-6 PM; Winter, 12 PM-5 PM
LOCATION: 11775 Watsonville Road, Gilroy
PHONE: 408-846-8463
WEBSITE: www.jstephens.com
GPS COORDINATES: 37.048763, -121.654908

6   Kirigin Cellars

The winery at Kirigin Cellars has had several owners since its founding in 1916, according to the winery's marketing director Maria Bruhns: "We are truly an international winery! Founded by Italians, sold to Croatians, currently owned by an Indian and we have a German winemaker!" As the oldest continually run winery in Gilroy, it is also one of the most interesting when it comes to history. For example, the house—which is just outside the tasting room and is now used as a private residence—was once the home of legendary "Cattle King" Henry Miller (1827-1916).

The Bonesio family was responsible for the winery's beginnings. Emigrating from Italy in 1916, Louis Bonesio and his family homesteaded the land and opened their winery. When Prohibition was enacted in 1919, the Bonesios officially produced sacramental wine, but

The entrance to Kirigin's tasting room is through old wine barrel doors.

also kept a secret wine cellar and would host bottle-your-own parties in the basement of their home during the 14 years the law was enforced. Another interesting tidbit is that Louis Bonesio was the first person in the world to live with organs from two separate donors (heart and kidney).

The Croatian part of this story enters with Nikola Kirigin-Chargin. Nikola made wine in his native Croatia until the Communist Yugoslav government seized his family's land. Along with his wife Birseka, they came to the U.S. in 1959. Nikola brought with him a degree in enology from the University of Zagreb (Croatia) and quickly found work as a winemaker in different parts of the U.S., including the Uvas Valley where the couple made their home. In 1976, Nikola was ready to retire when he learned that Louis Bonesio wanted to sell his winery. Having desired Bonesio's property for years because it reminded him of his mother country, Nikola bought the winery and renamed the winery Kirigin Cellars.

In following Maria's remarks about the winery's varied heritage, her German reference pertains to Kirigin's winemaker Allen Kreutzer. Growing weary from the demanding physical aspects of winemaking, Nikola hired Allen in 1985 and he has been with Kirigin since. (Allen is also the owner of Drytown Cellars in California's Sierra foothills.)

Fifteen years after hiring Allen, Nikola, then age 84, started thinking about retirement again. That's when he met Dhruv Khanna. Dhruv came to the U.S. from New Delhi, India, to attend Stanford Law School. A successful telecommunications attorney and the founder of Covad—a nationwide broadband company—Dhruv loved the game of cricket. Wanting to build a cricket pitch (field), he happened upon Kirigin Cellars' unfarmed 11 acres in 2000 and knew the level land would be perfect. Nikola sold the winery and land to Dhruv. "He wasn't actually looking to buy a winery," Maria said about Dhruv while showing us the beautifully developed and maintained field right next to the winery. "For Dhruv, cricket has taken a backseat. He's all about the wine now."

WINE MYTH "You have to know something about wine to enjoy it."
                                            — *Maria Bruhns*

Kirigin's wine offerings are vast and varied. The most interesting is their flagship wine "Vino de Mocca." The coffee- and chocolate-infused port is so special that its recipe is patented. Referred to as "The Kissing Wine," Nikola created it just for his wife, but it was Birseka (which means "pearl" in Croatian) who spirited its special love powers to others, giving bottles to couples who have difficulty conceiving. The results have been good—to see for yourself, check out the baby photos over the cash register!

Entering the driveway onto Kirigin's property, turn right at the fork and head around behind the house. You can't miss the tasting room entrance—an 1880s redwood fermentation tank doubles as the front doors and nearly the entire entry is covered in ivy and dwarfed by an overzealous tree. Don't be surprised if Kirigin's winery dog Jay runs out to greet you, because that's his job. An active Border Collie, he'll hit you up for a game of fetch with his favorite old cork. And if you've brought your pooch, know that Kirigin is a dog-friendly winery. "Your dog is welcome to stretch all fours on the fields," offered Maria.

FEATURED WINE: Malvasia Bianca, Cabernet Sauvignon, Zinfandel and dessert blends
TASTING COST: Complimentary
HOURS: Daily, 10 AM-5 PM
LOCATION: 11550 Watsonville Road, Gilroy
PHONE: 408-847-8827
WEBSITE: www.kirigincellars.com
GPS COORDINATES: 37.046528, -121.653357

7   Martin Ranch Winery

When Dan and Therese Martin opened their winery in 2002, this husband-and-wife winemaking team decided to create their own individual wine labels. For Therese, she chose "Therese Vineyards" for her wine label, and Dan, "JD Hurley." While the former name is self-explanatory, the latter requires elaboration: the "J" is for Dan's great-uncle Jack Hurley and the "D" for Jack's brother Dan Hurley. "Jack lived to be 107 years old," Dan shared. "The brand image on the label is the brand he used for his dairy in Salinas. He was my mentor when it came to farming, and he was a great human being."

Farming runs deep in both families. Dan's roots come from the

Dan and Therese enjoy the swings overlooking the vineyard's large pond.

Carmel Valley, where the original Martin Ranch was established, and Dan is the former owner of the local grocery chain Harvest Moon Markets. That's where he met Therese. Born and reared in the Santa Cruz Mountains area with an agricultural ancestry out of Corralitos, Therese worked for Dan for eight years until they married in 1991. Their home and site of their winery—appropriately named Martin Ranch—encompasses 17 acres of prime land. Following their collective love of fine wine, together they planted vineyards in 1993.

"Farming was the main reason for getting into the business," Therese said, noting they sold fruit to other wineries in the beginning, while still operating the grocery stores. "Then we had that 'ah-ha' moment in 1997: we couldn't sell our grapes. We had a 40-ton harvest and people were backing out of their buying commitments," she recalled, noting that in 1997 there was a glut of grapes in the market. So they took a ton of fruit to a friend who was a home winemaker and asked him to show them how to make wine. "We learned by trial and error," Therese mused, explaining that they eventually took enology classes at the University of California at Davis. In 2002, the Martins successfully launched their commercial wine business.

Following the tenets of tradition, passion and excellence, the dynamic duo has, over the course of a few short years, created wines worthy of all three doctrines. Today, eight different varietals can be found on their property. Regarding their dual roles as winemakers and winery owners, Dan confided, "I'm the grower and Therese is the lab tech. She does all the analyzing and decides when to harvest certain blocks."

Joking that Therese usually has to hold him back because he's anxious to get the fruit out of the field, Dan did give Therese many kudos, especially during harvest time when she oversees the picking crew. When asked who is right when it comes to certain winemaking decisions, Dan answered, "She has her own ideas and I have mine. On her wines, she's not willing to compromise that much!" To learn more about this winemaking couple, read their interview at **www.WineWherever.com.**

Being true to the environment is important to the Martins, and being green is their lifestyle, especially when it comes to the winery. For example, Dan designed the winery building using energy-saving techniques. He estimates they save more than 30 percent in electricity costs. The couple has initiated recycling programs to include a public collection point for used cork and wine bottles, as well as donating used wine barrels to local artisans for artistic endeavors. Their pond collects enough water during the winter to cover 90 percent of their watering needs for the vineyards. If that's not enough, Martin Ranch Winery is also a certified wildlife habitat, named as such on the National Wildlife Federation's registry.

The aforementioned one-acre lake, found north of the winery in the upper vineyard, is the place to be for the Martin's annual fishing derby. Open to wine club members, the summer event is the highlight of the year. Even though the lake is stocked with large-mouth bass, Dave admitted he doesn't fish that often. And that's too bad, as Therese is a gourmet cook; many of her recipes are listed on the winery's website under "Therese's Kitchen."

When heading to Martin Ranch, be sure to pay attention to the turn-off; the Y-shaped intersection of Redwood Retreat and Mt. Madonna roads can be confusing. Heading northwest on Redwood Retreat Road, bear right at the Y. If you miss the crossroad, you'll find yourself at the beginning of Mt. Madonna Road. The winery is about 3.5 miles from the intersection.

FEATURED WINE: Cabernet Sauvignon, Syrah, Sangiovese and Sauvignon Blanc
TASTING COST: $10, returned with $20 purchase
HOURS: Third weekend of the month, 12 PM-5 PM
LOCATION: 6675 Redwood Retreat Road, Gilroy
PHONE: 408-842-9197
WEBSITE: www.martinranchwinery.com
GPS COORDINATES: 37.036804, -121.712646

Gilroy

8 Sarah's Vineyard

Sarah's Vineyard, found at the eastern foot of Mt. Madonna in the shadow of the Santa Cruz Mountains, is the pride of owner Tim Slater, a self-described "mad scientist." Before we explain this, here's a quick history of the winery. Marilyn Clark founded it in 1978, naming it "Sarah's Vineyard." The story goes that Sarah R. Bunning settled on the property in the mid-1950s with her family. When Marilyn acquired the property over 25 years later, she strongly felt that the essence of Sarah remained in the land. Naming her winery "Sarah's Vineyard" seemed the right thing to do—immortalizing Sarah's name and spirit.

Prior to Tim getting involved in the wine business, he was an extremely busy and successful Silicon Valley engineer who was growing tired of his frenzied lifestyle. In 2001, he met Marilyn by happenstance. She, too, was weary of her job running the day-to-day operations of a winery. Each facing a similar lifestyle roadblock, they decided to help each other and Tim purchased Sarah's Vineyard from Marilyn.

"Marilyn, an eclectic mystic, was one of the earliest proponents

of organic and biodynamic farming for wine grapes," said Tim, noting that the vineyard was one of the original boutique wineries of the late 1970s and early '80s. He added that Marilyn had created "a sustainable farming heritage we continue to this day."

Sarah's Vineyard is comprised of 16 acres and hosts eight varietals, including their flagships Pinot Noir and Chardonnay. "We recently introduced a lineup of estate Rhone varietals and Chateauneuf-du-Pape inspired blends, with Viognier, Roussanne, Marsanne, Grenache Blanc, Grenache and Counoise planted on the property in 2004 and

2006," Tim noted. Because the vineyard is tucked into a small dell near a windy mountain pass, Tim explained that the microclimate for his grapes is maritime in nature; a typical summer day begins with morning fog, followed by full sunlight moderated by ocean breezes, ending with chilly nights—all ideal conditions for growing premium fruit. Ken Deis—a 40-year winemaking veteran most noted for helping create the modern Napa Valley wine industry—is Sarah's Vineyard's winemaker.

It's a good bet that Tim is right there with Ken during the winemaking process, referring to his "mad scientist" label—and that's mad crazy, not mad angry. Tim really is a scientist and also an engineer and a prolific inventor with over 25 patents in the field of "micromachining." Examples given for his work in the Silicon Valley include creating artificial retinas for vision restoration in the blind, large-scale optical networking equipment and micro-satellite thermal controllers.

The winery's tasting room is located on the back of the property. Enter the driveway, head up the hill, then to the right and around to the backside. The tasting room, which opened in 2003, is an old—but restored—horse barn, and parts of the wood floor are original. Their picnic grounds, which include a deck and bocce ball courts, overlook the West Side Nursery. Inside, besides being treated to great wine by a great staff, you'll also see a small gallery with rotating exhibits by local artists.

FEATURED WINE: Pinot Noir, Chardonnay, Syrah and Zinfandel
TASTING COST: $5
HOURS: Daily, 11 AM-5 PM
LOCATION: 4005 Hecker Pass Road, Gilroy
PHONE: 408-847-1947
WEBSITE: www.sarahsvineyard.com
GPS COORDINATES: 37.013709, -121.645056

Gilroy

9 Satori Cellars

While researching this book, it was not uncommon for us to visit more than a dozen wineries a day. Since most of our trips stretched over several days, this nonstop activity would at times become so grueling that we actually looked forward to collapsing on a lumpy hotel room bed and eating dinner from the vending machine.

The day we visited Satori was no different. It was an unusually warm March afternoon and we were worn out from running between

Owners Sandy and Tom Moller in their Satori Cellars' open-air tasting room.

wineries all day long. Turning onto Buena Vista Avenue, we spotted Satori Cellars and the many cars parked out front. At first we thought we were interrupting a private event, but soon learned that their vernal equinox party, marking the first day of spring, was in full swing. The place was jammed with festive wine lovers, a live band was performing and the wine was flowing. An outside bar—which turned out to be their permanent tasting bar—was packed. One guy in a bright purple T-shirt that read "Law and Order: New York City" seemed to be thoroughly enjoying himself, visiting with everyone. We asked him if owner Tom Moller were available. He grinned and said he was Tom.

Buddy, one of the Satori wine dogs

Amid all the festivities, Tom was the host of hosts. He took us on tour and told us about his business. When asked about the winery's name, Tom explained that he came upon it while meditating, using the first two letters from his name, his wife Sandy's name and son Riley's name. He then Googled the word "satori" and learned that it meant "sudden unbidden moments of absolute stillness and peace in which time stops and the perfection and beauty of creation shine forth." Later that day, while reading Eckhart Tolle's book, *The Power of Now*, the same word popped out of the text. "Tolle described it as a 'taste of enlightenment,'" Tom said. "It was meant to be."

The same might be said for how Tom became a winery owner and winemaker. As a radio frequency engineer, he never had such a career change in the plans. But the universe had other ideas for Tom. He had formed a small design group for Ericsson in 1990, at the infancy of cell phone development. Starting with fewer than a dozen people, by the time the cell phone boom hit, his group exploded into a multinational division with over $250 million in sales and 1,000 employees on the payroll. Tom has 11 patents in his name, all in the field of high-powered radio frequency electronics; the next time you make a call on your cell, you can thank Tom. (To learn more about Tom and Sandy, read the rest of their interview at **www.WineWherever.com**.)

While he was still involved in the high-tech industry, Tom purchased a 20-acre parcel that included a small house and a dying plum orchard that dated back to the 1940s. A gentleman farmer, Tom was not sure what to do with the land. He had tried planting Christmas trees, but that didn't work out because of the absence of an irrigation system! Frustrated, Tom listened when a friend who was a home winemaker suggested he plant a vineyard. So in 1999 he did. Spending time in the vineyard and learning about winemaking, Tom became hooked. He learned as much as he could from other winemakers, books and

> **WINE MYTH** "Winemakers actually make wine; it's Mother Nature who makes the wine." — *Tom Moller*

classes at the University of California at Davis. In 2006, he retired from the high tech world to focus on Satori.

The slogan for Satori Cellars is "Celebrating the Journey." Today, with 15 acres of vineyard and a successful winery behind them, the Mollers enjoy their adventure. Their bold wines have done well, especially their "Hallelujah Cabernet Sauvignon" which has won many awards, including a double gold at the *San Francisco Chronicle* Wine Competition.

Satori Cellar's tasting room is located outdoors under a large covered alcove overlooking a lavender-rosemary labyrinth. We loved the Zen/Mother Earth theme, which at the time of our visit seemed very relevant because of the celebration taking place. But in visiting with Tom and Sandy, we saw the evidence of their united commitment to their business and the earth. Regardless whether you show up for one of their great equinox or solstice parties or casually drop by on Saturday or Sunday, the Mollers will invite you to celebrate their journey with them—over a glass of Satori Cellars wine, of course!

FEATURED WINE: Zinfandel, Cabernet Sauvignon, Merlot and Petite Sirah
TASTING COST: $7, applied to wine purchase
HOURS: Saturday and Sunday, 12 PM-5 PM
LOCATION: 2100 Buena Vista Avenue, Gilroy
PHONE: 408-848-5823
WEBSITE: www.satoricellars.com
GPS COORDINATES: 37.051733, -121.550024

Gilroy

10 Solis Winery

Vic and Mike Vanni are the owners of Solis Winery. Named after the historic Rancho de Solis—an 1830s' Mexican land grant that once included more than 8,500 acres—the original winery dates to 1917. David Vanni, the boys' father, opened Solis Winery in 1989. A first-generation American born in San Francisco, David was the son of hard-working Italian immigrants who owned a cut-flower business in Mountain View in the 1940s. David grew up in the business, taking over later.

In 1980, David moved his young family to Gilroy to be closer to their second flower nursery in nearby Watsonville. It was then David purchased a small five-acre vineyard on Hecker Pass Highway, next to Bertero Winery, taking the grapes home to make wine in the family basement. During that time, Bertero sold and became Summerhill Vineyards, but went out of business in 1988. Soon after, David purchased the winery and in 1989, he and his new wife Valerie opened their winery.

During their years growing up, sons Vic and Mike were involved in the family flower business. But as young men often do, they both set out to forge their own paths. Vic worked in commercial real estate and Mike in a potted plant nursery and at Bonfante Gardens (now Gilroy Gardens). When their father and stepmom decided to sell the winery in 2007, both boys came home. "Mike and I did not come directly to the winery; we both made long trips to it," concluded Vic. Today, Mike takes care of the front end of the business, concentrating on vineyard management, overall winery maintenance, winemaking and inventory, while Vic oversees sales, accounting, special events, compliance, marketing and the tasting room.

Solis Winery has 16 acres of vineyard on site and another 30 acres off site. They specialize in Chardonnay, Merlot, Muscat Canelli, Johannesburg Riesling, Cabernet Sauvignon and Sangiovese, several of which have won the California State Fair's "Best of Class of Region" award for three years in a row. They also feature another unusual varietal—Fiano. A strong-flavored white grape native to southern Italy, the varietal has been cultivated in Sicily for more than two thousand years. According to Vic, there are only a handful of Fiano growers and producers in the state. "It is nice to have a unique product, because people are always intrigued. But we find that most people, despite themselves, stick with what they know and are reluctant to try something new," he shared, noting that maybe someday Solis will put Fiano "on the map."

And there's no doubt this dynamic brotherly duo can achieve this dream. Agriculture and hard work run in the Vanni blood. "Most of my life was spent on the vineyard or at the nursery, so agriculture is all I really know," Vic said. "Hard work was the strongest virtue, according to my dad, so we didn't sit around much." Vic went on to obtain a bachelor's in agricultural business at California Polytechnic State University in San Luis Obispo. Mike attended the same college, graduating with a degree in agricultural engineering technology. Both men have children, seven total to date. "Like our parents, we want to see our kids understand the concept of hard work, but to also enjoy what they do. We have made a commitment to see them grow up intrigued with the business, and our hope is to pass the winery on to them," confided Vic.

We loved the tasting room at Solis, mainly because the set-up is so different. Walking up the steps to the covered front porch of what looks to be an old ranch home, you enter the building and descend into the tasting room via short staircases on either side. Once downstairs, the tasting bar is a circular shape, with a black leather bar bumper and brass foot rail. In back is a large deck overlooking their gorgeous vineyard and the mountains beyond; here you can relax with a glass of exceptional Solis wine.

FEATURED WINE: Fiano, Sangiovese, Merlot and Syrah
TASTING COST: $5
HOURS: Daily, 12 PM-5 PM
LOCATION: 3920 Hecker Pass Road, Gilroy
PHONE: 408-847-6306
WEBSITE: www.soliswinery.com
GPS COORDINATES: 37.013341, -121.639874

11 Thomas Kruse Winery

If you desire a genuine rural wine tasting experience, look no further than Thomas Kruse Winery. The drive to the winery took us along rural country roads and past small ranch homes. Pulling into the driveway, we found the tasting room to the left and the residence nearby. Vineyards were everywhere, nestled up against green rolling hills, and the tasting room shared space with the winery, barrel room and storage area. There is absolutely nothing pretentious about this winery, and we imagine that's perfectly fine with owner Thomas "Tom" Kruse.

Tom grew up in Chicago and came to this area in his early twenties. Having spent summers on a farm when he was younger, he purchased an antique basket press, similar to ones used to make hard cider on the old farm. But forget the apples—his buddies talked him into using grapes instead. The grape experiment was successful, much to

Tom Kruse enjoys hands-on work in his vineyard.

everyone's surprise, and Tom was hooked. He spent time learning everything he could about winemaking, fermentation science and grape growing, even opening a store for home winemakers where he taught wine appreciation classes. In 1970, Tom and his wife Karen found the current property, which hosted an old barn and small house. In 1971, the couple opened their winery. To date, Thomas Kruse Winery is the longest continuously operating, federally licensed sole proprietorship in the nation.

> **WINE MYTH** "Corks breathe." — *Tom Kruse*

What's interesting about this winery is that besides the help of family, the Kruses depend greatly on volunteers to run the business. The tasting room is open six days a week and is staffed by volunteers

Tom demonstrates an old sparkling wine corking machine.

who each work a day in exchange for a case of wine. Tom said the volunteers are "wonderful folks who enjoy this connection with the winery. Of course, if we have something else going on, they pitch in with that also." The one rule Tom has when it comes to volunteering is that he never wants the work to become drudgery, so typically each volunteer works only one day a month.

The year 2010 marks Tom's fortieth crush. Over all those years, Tom has done just about anything and everything when it comes to the wine business, including making dry Rosés from uncommon varietals such as Carignane and Grignolino to being the first winemaker ever to "label" Thompson Seedless wine. When asked about the allure of taking a standard table grape and making wine, Tom had ulterior motives. "Before the government required a varietal to be 75 percent of the variety [a requirement per labeling rules], it only used to have to be 51 percent. I saw that the total amount of tons of Thompson Seedless crushed by wineries exceeded the total of all the other varieties combined," Tom said, thinking back to 1975 or thereabouts. "It was apparent that people were drinking Thompson Seedless grapes as 49 percent of many of the wines they were drinking. This prompted me to do one as a spoof on the industry." Tom laughed, adding, "It was good, by  the way." To learn more about Tom, check out his interview at **www. WineWherever.com.**

Tom's great sense of humor runs in the family. The couple's son Peter—now a winemaker at Roche Winery in Sonoma County—cut his teeth on winemaking through the family business. One story Tom recounted was about the family labeling thousands of bottles, all by hand, and what a very young Peter thought of the chore: "When he was putting on the capsules [foil enclosure that covers the cork], he wrote a little note and put it in the capsule before he put it on the bottle. It said, 'Help, I'm being held prisoner by this winery!' A customer brought it back to show us and inquire as to Peter's welfare!"

Keeping in mind that the winery is small and depends on volunteers when busy, the Kruses ask that reservations be made for groups of ten or more. They also ask that visitors drive slowly into their place, as many animals are around, including their winery dog Millie.

FEATURED WINE: Cabernet Sauvignon, Merlot, Chardonnay and Zinfandel
TASTING COST: Complimentary
HOURS: Tuesday-Sunday, 12 PM-5 PM
LOCATION: 3200 Dryden Avenue, Gilroy
PHONE: 408-842-7458
WEBSITE: www.thomaskrusewinery.com
GPS COORDINATES: 37.042209, -121.52439

Los Gatos

12 Fleming Jenkins Vineyards & Winery

We looked forward to our trip to Los Gatos. Its pedestrian-friendly downtown area—where the tasting room for Fleming Jenkins Vineyards & Winery is located—is a great stop when visiting the Santa Cruz Mountain region. Upon our arrival, we sneaked in the back door since the tasting room hadn't opened yet. Greg Jenkins and his staff greeted us warmly, and it was wonderful to have the owner/winemaker all to ourselves before opening time. His wife—Olympic gold medalist Peggy Fleming—wasn't there, but just up the hill at their Los Gatos home. "We've lived in this community for over 30 years," Greg said.

(Photo courtesy of Fleming Jenkins Vineyards & Winery)

"Having our tasting room here is important to us."

As with everything this couple does—from Greg's 30 years as a successful dermatologist to Peggy's ice skating and television career—commitment, perseverance and patience are key. The same elements are needed to start a winery, including a little faith and a lot of hard work, as the couple would learn. Wanting to add some landscaping to a side yard in 1999, Greg and Peggy decided to go with a vineyard. Chardonnay was planted and over the next few years, Greg continued his medical practice while tending to their grapes.

When the couple was younger, Greg had made wine in the garage of their San Francisco home. Now having his own vineyard, he became enthralled with the thought of opening a winery. To learn more about the craft, Greg asked winemaking friends for guidance and also took classes at the University of California at Davis. Having a science and chemistry background was a big plus. "There's an art and science to medicine and there's an art and science to winemaking as well," Greg determined. "You have to apply the right thing at the right time."

Yes, timing is everything, and this fairly young winery, which opened in 2003, is receiving much acclaim. For example, their wine "Victories Rosé" was awarded the number-two spot for its price range in *Wine Spectator* with a score of 89 points (July 2010). Remember: this is for a Rosé, and an important one at that. "Peggy is a breast cancer survivor, so when we started making Rosé, we said, 'Hey—pink wine, pink ribbon!' It was a natural fit," beamed Greg. For every bottle sold, an average of $2 is donated to breast cancer research. Since the wine's release in 2004, more than $30,000 has been donated. "This wine really pays tribute to victories that people go through in life, whether they are facing adversity or are part of the support team. Everyone has victories in life to celebrate," Greg added.

Greg found that he can't make great wine from anything less than great grapes. For this reason, he uses only the best selections from certain vineyards, including the couple's Chardonnay estate vineyard along with that of football legend and Hall of Famer John Madden, whose personal 200-acre vineyard is located in the Livermore valley. Peggy met John when she became stranded on the east coast during 9/11. Getting word from his agent that she was stuck, John, who lives in the Bay Area but happened to be on the East Coast at the time, gave her a lift home in his luxury bus. After two days on the road, Peggy and John formed a fast friendship. It's a great story, so be sure to ask tasting room staff for details when you visit.

Fleming Jenkins' production facility is found at Los Gatos' historic Novitiate Winery. A former Jesuit winery for nearly 100 years, the winery is now home to Testarossa Winery (see page 120). "The opportunity to work closely with Testarossa gives us the ability to frequently compare notes with their talented winemaker Bill Brosseau and proprietors Rob and Diana Jensen," said Greg. To learn more about Greg, read his interview at **www.WineWherever.com**.

As you would expect, the tasting room fits in beautifully with

---

WINE MYTH "You have to finish a bottle of red wine on the same day it's opened." — *Greg Jenkins*

---

the charm of downtown Los Gatos. From their knotty pine floor to their luxurious tasting counter manned by knowledgeable and friendly staffers, there's a lot to see and experience at Fleming Jenkins. And, of course, for you Peggy fans (who isn't?), memorabilia from her ice skating career is on display, including the chartreuse-colored outfit she wore when she won the gold medal for figure skating at the 1968 Winter Olympics in Grenoble, France. You can also purchase Peggy's autobiography, *The Long Program*; for each book sold, $5 is donated to the Sobrato Cancer Center, a clinic of the Santa Clara Valley Medical Center. If you happen to visit when Peggy is there (she helps out when it's busy), she would love to autograph her book for you.

FEATURED WINE: Chardonnay, Syrah, Rosé and a Cabernet blend
TASTING COST: $10, of which $5 is refunded for each bottle purchased
HOURS: Tuesday-Sunday, 12 PM-6 PM
LOCATION: 45 W. Main Street, Los Gatos
PHONE: 408-358-4949
WEBSITE: www.flemingjenkins.com
GPS COORDINATES: 37.221842, -121.982637

13 Testarossa Winery

R ob and Diana Jensen both honor a strong faith in each other and in the American Dream. They met in the 1980s when they were both taking electrical engineering classes at Santa Clara University, a Jesuit school. They married in 1988, but not before Rob, who was also earning a minor in Italian and Italian culture, spent two summers studying abroad in the central Italian hill town of Assisi. While there, Rob—a redhead—was given the nickname "Testarossa" which means "redhead" in Italian.

Living in Sunnyvale, the Jensens both worked in the high-tech industry for several years. But their love of food and wine had them making their first batch of home wine in the early 1990s. By 1994,

Testarossa's grand stone entry sets the stage for their expansive tasting room.

they were averaging 200 cases "which launched us into the wine business," shared Diana. "We decided that we wanted to turn our hobby into our living." She left her job in 1994 to manage their new business and raise the couple's first child Nick, born in 1993, and then Claire, who came along in 1996. Rob continued working his Silicon Valley job for several years, finally hanging up his IPO hat in 2001 to work at the winery full time.

> **WINE MYTH** "Wine connoisseurs only drink red wine." — *Diana Jensen*

Determined to realize their dream of becoming winery owners, together the couple took every viticulture and enology class offered through the extension program at the University of California at Davis. They planted dozens of grapevines in their yard. They also befriended the late Tom Mudd, owner of Cinnabar Winery (see page 138) and Cinnabar's winemaker George Troquato. Both men took the fledging winemakers under their wings and taught them well. Eager students, the Jensens leased a 1.5-acre vineyard at the urging of George and spent the next five years tending to the vines with the help of many friends and family. Needing money to fund vineyard improvements, they sold "futures" (speculating on future wine releases) to friends for their 1994 release. The offer became so popular they had to source fruit from other vineyards. In 1994, Tom leased space to the couple at his winery, where the senior winemaker George helped the Jensens create several releases.

By 1996, the couple had outgrown their space at Cinnabar. That's when George literally pushed them out of the nest, telling them about the historic 19th century Novitiate (pronounced no-vish-ut) Winery in Los Gatos. Having a strong Jesuit background, Rob and Diana knew it was meant to be. The winery was originally built in 1888 by northern Italian Jesuit priests and was the funding source for their seminary college. The winery closed in 1986, just two years shy of its 100th birthday. Subsequently, several vintners leased the property beginning in 1986, including the Jensens in 1997.

More than a decade later, the Jensens are living the American Dream. Under the watchful gaze and magical touch of winemaker Bill Brosseau, many have praised Testarossa wine. "We are viewed by the major wine critics as one of the top-rated Pinot Noir and Chardon-

nay producers in California," Diana said. Another award-winning winery—Fleming Jenkins Vineyards & Winery (see page 117)—leases production space from the facility.

Testarossa's tasting room opened in 2003. The winery and tasting room are found on a hill overlooking Los Gatos. Heading up the hill and through the residential area can be confusing, but follow the "Novitiate Historic Winery" signs and you'll get there just fine. Once on the grounds, continue around the bend where you'll find parking. Once you park, walk toward the eastern side of the building, the side facing the wooded park setting (if you continue up the hill, you'll find yourself on the Jesuit campus). The entrance to the tasting room is awe-inspiring. You'll walk through a grand-looking stone cave lined with historic photos from the winery's heyday. Once inside, you'll be surprised by the vast size of the tasting room and adjoining facilities. Testarossa's wine list is huge, one of the most ample we found in our research; be sure to try their Niclaire Pinot Noir, named for their children Nick and Claire.

FEATURED WINE: Chardonnay, Pinot Noir and Syrah
TASTING COST: $10
HOURS: Daily, 11 AM-5 PM
LOCATION: 300-A College Avenue, Los Gatos
PHONE: 408-354-6150
WEBSITE: www.testarossa.com
GPS COORDINATES: 37.214028, -121.980733

14 Castillo's Hillside Shire Winery

When Jess and Roni Jo Castillo purchased 11.5 acres of prime Morgan Hill land in 1997 to build their dream home, little did they know that a 1960s-era Kern County assemblyman by the name of John Williamson would turn their world upside down and force them into the wine business.

The Castillo's plan was to tear down an old farmhouse on the property and build an 8,000-square-foot English-manor home. They were owners of a very successful construction business, but when it came time for the Castillos to pull the building permits, they got caught up in the California Land Conservation Act of 1965, better known by the author's name—the Williamson Act. Originally created

The "members-only" lounge (Photo courtesy of Castillo's Hillside Shire Winery)

to give farmers tax breaks in lieu of them selling their agriculture land to big developers, the act has many requirements. "We were told that in order to build on any land over 10 acres, we had to make a living from some form of agriculture generated by the land," said Roni Jo.

After days of worry and exasperation, the Castillo's decided to plant grapes on their very steep hillside and open a winery. The crazy thing about their decision is that neither Jess nor Roni Jo drank wine and they knew nothing about the business. "Never in our wildest dreams did we think we would become grape growers and winery owners," laughed Roni Jo. "When we got our first batch into the barrels, the smell was horrible. I thought, 'Oh my God! I have to smell this stench for the rest of my life?' But now it's a beautiful smell and I love it!"

Eight acres of estate Cabernet Sauvignon and Petite Sirah grace

Castillo's Hillside Shire Winery tasting room

the land behind their home. The hillside is so steep that workers must tie themselves to poles at the top and rappel down to the vines. And they augment their grape needs by purchasing fruit from other vineyards. "We blend the wine that blends people!" Roni Jo said. Jess is the winemaker and gets help, when required, from a wine consultant. The couples' three adult children also help: Michael works the construction side of the business with his father but helps out with crush; son Nate works in the tasting room and outside sales; and daughter Vivienne—the artist of the family—designs their Harlequin-themed labels, works in the tasting room and entertains guests by singing and playing the guitar.

During our visit with the Castillos, Roni Jo led us into their

---

WINE MYTH "Red with beef, white with fish." — *Roni Jo Castillo*

"members-only" lounge. Located to the right of their home, the lounge is an exquisite two-story English cottage with a gnarly pepper tree at the entrance and a lake behind. We became spellbound as we crossed over the threshold; it was as if we were entering a hobbit's home. Inside, the impeccably-dressed Roni Jo fussed with what she called "her mess"—even though she is a hypnotherapist, her flair for interior decorating was highly evident in the beautiful swaths of fabric strewn about and also the cottage's motif. Moving everything out of the way, Roni Jo excitedly showed us plans for their future tasting room, which will be modeled after the famed 12th century Siena Duomo, a cathedral in Sienna, Italy. "Wow." That's all we could say. No doubt that whatever the Castillos set their mind to, they will be successful.

From there, the three of us walked downhill to the Castillo's current tasting room, enjoying the view of the valley along the way. Here we found a colorful Harlequin figure painted on the floor and bits of matching whimsy throughout. And the official winery animals greeted us: Gordy, the lively Border Collie; Haley, the lovable Shepherd mix; and Chris Farley, a chubby chunk of a cat who plopped down at our feet and insisted on being loved.

Castillo's Hillside Shire Winery is literally at the end of East Main Street where the road runs into the foothills. When the gate is open, pull straight into their small parking lot.

FEATURED WINE: Petite Syrah, Sangiovese, Syrah and Cabernet Sauvignon
TASTING COST: $5
HOURS: Saturday, 12 PM-7 PM; Sunday, 12 PM-5 PM
LOCATION: 2215 Liberata Drive, Morgan Hill
PHONE: 408-595-3145
WEBSITE: www.castilloshillsideshirewinery.com
GPS COORDINATES: 37.15288, -121.623015

Morgan Hill

15 Guglielmo Winery

Guglielmo Winery is one of the oldest wineries in the Santa Clara Valley. Founded in 1925, the Morgan Hill winery is now run by a third generation of Guglielmos.

Founder Emilio Guglielmo (pronounced Gool-yell-mo) immigrated to America in 1908 from the Piedmonte region of Italy. Only 25 years old when he arrived in New York, Emilio headed to the Oklahoma Territory where he had work waiting for him. Two years later, he found himself in San Francisco. Once settled, he sent for his Piedmonte sweetheart Emilia and the couple married as soon as she arrived. While in San Francisco, Emilio, who came from a long line of Italian winemakers, made wine for friends and neighbors.

Looking for an opportunity to make a new life in America,

Emilio and Emilia worked hard and saved money to purchase land for a vineyard. Their dream came true in 1925 when the couple acquired the property where the winery stands today. Since Prohibition was in effect at the time, Emilio made wine for churches, but had regular customers, too, making his wine in a hidden cellar underneath the family home. Today, the home serves as the winery's business office and is the building to your left as you head to the tasting room. And yes, the hidden cellar is still there, barrels and all.

WINE MYTH "Smelling the cork in a restaurant will tell you if the wine is bad." — *George Guglielmo*

When Prohibition was lifted in 1933, the Guglielmos were well positioned to immediately get their wine out to the elated wine-drinking masses. Focusing their sales on the huge population base in San Francisco, the couple sold their Italian wines to Italian, French and Basque communities, as well as to many of the city's finest restaurants. The Guglielmo name quickly became synonymous with quality, and the winery realized enormous success.

In the late 1940s, the winery was passed down to Emilio's son, George W. Guglielmo. Along with his wife Madeline, George continued building the estate vineyards and broadening their distribution channels. The couple had three boys: George E., Gene and Gary. Today, all three men are carrying on the family tradition of creating premium wine. George E. is the winemaker and oversees the growing of the grapes in the vineyard and all aspects of wine production. Gene is the director of sales, and Gary is the general manager.

As winemaker, George is continuing the Guglielmo winemaking tradition passed down from his ancestors in Northern Italy. Considered the heart and soul of Guglielmo Winery, a young George spent countless hours with his father and grandfather Emilio working side-by-side in the vineyards and winery. When he's not cooking gourmet meals or tinkering with his 1957 cherry-red Chevy Cameo pickup—originally purchased by Grandfather Emilio—George is at the winery, producing three different labels: Guglielmo Private Reserve, their newest brand "TRÉ" and their oldest label "Emile's." (In French, Emilio is Emile.) "It's our family's strong belief that wines should be easy for everyone to enjoy at a reasonable price," George said. The winery releases upwards of 40,000 cases of wine annually.

The vineyards of Guglielmo are made up of Zinfandel, Petite Sirah and Grignolino, a red Italian grape varietal from the northwestern corner of Italy—the Piedmont region—and more importantly, Emilio's homeland. The grapes are typically used when producing light-colored wines and Rosés. The family makes limited amounts of this varietal under the name "Rosatello." The winery believes that only one other winery in the state is producing the rare wine varietal.

The tasting room at Guglielmo Winery is wonderful and fun.

Remember, they have been wine tasting on the property since 1934, so they know how to take care of their customers! In the late 1960s, the family transformed their original winery barn into their tasting room. The bar itself is beyond delightful, and the original stonewalls and wooden beams above give you the flavor of a bygone era. While in the tasting room, be sure to walk all the way to the back of the building to view old Guglielmo family photos.

Outside, you'll find a village fountain in a cobblestone piazza, as well as old farm equipment on display with interpretive signs. To the left of the winery is the elegant Villa Emile Event Center, the perfect place to rent for your special occasion.

FEATURED WINE: Zinfandel, Petite Sirah, Cabernet Sauvignon and Sangiovese
TASTING COST: $5
HOURS: Daily, 10 AM-5 PM
LOCATION: 1480 East Main Avenue, Morgan Hill
PHONE: 408-779-2145
WEBSITE: www.guglielmowinery.com
GPS COORDINATES: 37.146288, -121.633987

Morgan Hill

16 Sycamore Creek
Vineyards
& Winery

Sycamore Creek Vineyards & Winery sits in the eastern foothills of
the Santa Cruz Mountains, west of the city of Morgan Hill. Located
on Uvas Road—a well-known and well-traveled country thoroughfare
in these parts that, at various points, runs alongside Uvas Creek and by
the Uvas Reservoir—the winery actually takes its name from another
small creek that bisects the property.

The word "uva" means "grape" in Spanish so, as the story goes,
early explorers named the valley where this winery is situated after the

native vines they found growing in the area. Uvas Creek, which draws from the Santa Cruz Mountains, runs the length of the valley before joining the Pajaro River by Gilroy, then draining into Monterey Bay. It was on this spot that the Marchetti family established their ranch at the beginning of the 20th century, planting head-pruned vineyards (no trellises) of Carignane and Zinfandel in 1917. Two years later, Prohibition came along and many of the vineyards were removed, but not all.

Not much is known about the vineyards from the beginning of Prohibition through 1975, with the exception that the Marchettis did farm their land during most of this time period. But beginning in 1975 and over the next 30 years, the Sycamore Creek Vineyard property and winery was sold several times, trading hands between a husband-and-wife set of schoolteachers and a Japanese businessman. Finally, in 2005, Bill and Carolyn Holt purchased the property, making their son-in-law Ted Medeiros general manager and winemaker. Ted previously had been involved in growing premium wine grapes for years at Uvas Creek Vineyards, located a mere half mile north of his in-law's new place.

Ted is a rarity—he's one of those self-taught winemakers. A fruit grower, he planted four Bordeaux varietals on his in-law's place, but soon realized that selling the huge lot of fruit was going to be more difficult than expected. "We were too small for the larger wineries and too pricey for most home winemakers," Ted explained. "That's when I decided to put up some of my own wine." And that's also when Ted got a crash course in winemaking. The story gets better. Instead of making just one wine, he made eight kinds of Cabernets, a Petit Verdot, a

Cabernet Franc and a Merlot, all using different techniques. Keep in mind that Ted had never made wine before this. "In essence, the first year I had 11 shots at it as well as the opportunity to see what worked. I took what worked and did the same thing the following year, making eight more Cabs and my first Blanc," Ted said. "So after two years, I had experienced what most winemakers take 20 years to learn. With a passion and some decent note taking, my learning curve was advanced because I was not afraid to screw something up in order to learn from it."

> **WINE MYTH** "There are no myths, it's all true!" — *Ted Medeiros*

And learn he did. This small family-owned and operated winery produces upwards of 3,500 cases of handcrafted estate wines per year. And when the Holts—who are turning over the winery to Ted and their daughter Tammie—found one remaining Zinfandel vine on their property soon after purchasing the place, they were thrilled. Here, next to Sycamore Creek, stood the sole survivor of the pre-Prohibition Marchetti vineyard. Ted took cuttings from the nearly 100-year-old struggling vine and grafted them to existing vines at the Uvas Creek Vineyard. The goal is to replant a portion of the Sycamore Creek with the original Zinfandel vine.

The winery's entrance off of Uvas Road will sneak up on you quickly, so watch for it. Upon entering the property, you'll drive over a short one-lane bridge that spans Sycamore Creek, the winery's namesake. From there, head up the small hill, between some field houses and a shed, and you'll find the tasting room straight ahead. More than likely, Syrah—their official wine dog—will meet you and lead you inside. A mixed-breed female, Syrah was abandoned on the property as a puppy and, as Ted jokes, she adopted the Medeiros family for her own, not the other way around!

FEATURED WINE: Cabernet Sauvignon, Petit Verdot and Bordeaux blends
TASTING COST: $5
HOURS: Thursday-Monday, 12 PM-5 PM
LOCATION: 12775 Uvas Road, Morgan Hill
PHONE: 408-779-4738
WEBSITE: www.sycamorecreekvineyards.com
GPS COORDINATES: 37.060167, -121.664298

17 J. Lohr Vineyards & Winery

After days of roaming the hills and mountains of the Mid-Coast, visiting quaint wineries in ranch-like settings, pulling into the urban parking lot of a San Jose-based winery felt rather odd at first, especially with a high school right across the street. The winery's brick building was unassuming on the outside, but what we found inside was wonderful—this is where the legacy of J. Lohr wines began.

The original operations center, this part of the J. Lohr dynasty is now called the "J. Lohr San Jose Wine Center." Our gracious hosts were Bill Flint, who has been with the company for 20 years, and marketing coordinator Megan Carder. Unfortunately, none of the Lohr family was available, even though we did have the honor of hanging out with Steve Lohr, oldest son of family patriarch and founder Jerry Lohr, at a Paso Robles wine event a few weeks later.

The Wine Center building has a fun history, as spirits have been brewed here for more than 150 years. The structure was built in 1856 and the last noted brewing company on record was Pacific Brewing and Malting—home of Wieland's Beer. In 1952, Pacific sold their huge plant to Falstaff Beer, marking the first time Falstaff had ever sold their beer in California. Even though Falstaff was the eighth most popular brewer in the nation at the time, in 1973 they closed the San Jose plant and moved production to their San Francisco brewery. The company eventually folded in 2005.

The closing of Falstaff's brewery in San Jose proved to be Jerry Lohr's gain. A South Dakota farm boy, Jerry's agricultural acumen led him to California in 1966 in search of the perfect place to start a vineyard. Traveling throughout the Golden State, he favored the Mid-Coast region and settled on land that eventually would become part of Monterey County's Arroyo Seco appellation. In 1972, Jerry and his eldest son Steve—who was only 10 years old—began planting their vineyard, 280 acres in all. While the vineyard matured, Jerry needed to find a production facility; the Falstaff plant was perfect, so he acquired it from the beer company. J. Lohr's first wine—a Petite Sirah—was released in 1974, the same year they opened their San Jose tasting room.

J. Lohr's San Jose Wine Center hasn't changed much in 37 years, with the exception of a remodel in 2003 to add an event room. Inside you'll find, as the company calls it, wine with "Flavor Second to None." The classy open-beam construction and polished woods throughout add to the great experience of enjoying their wine. "Visitors can almost receive a mini-course in Central Coast varietals," Megan said, referring to what guests can expect when they visit either the San Jose Wine Center or its sister wine center in Paso Robles. With approximately 3,700 acres of vineyards in Monterey County's Arroyo Seco region, Paso Robles and Napa Valley's St. Helena, their wine varietals run the gamut from Cabernet to Chardonnay to Valdiguié, a red grape originating in the Languedoc-Roussillon region of southern France, sometimes referred to as Gamay.

Many surprises await wine lovers when they visit J. Lohr. One is an exclusive indulgence—the invitation to taste one of the limited-release wines from the J. Lohr "Gesture" wine label. Made only for tasting room guests and wine club members, the Rhone-inspired varietals and blends come from their Paso Robles and Monterey vineyards.

Another surprise has to do with mechanization and speed. In a room just off the tasting area, you can sip your wine and get a behind-the-scenes look at J. Lohr's bottling line in full production. We were mesmerized by the activity, as only a pane of glass separated us

---

WINE MYTH "A winery with large volume production cannot make wines with a hand-crafted touch." — *Cynthia Lohr*

---

from conveyor belts that whizzed by with endless wine bottles. And we watched as huge machines quickly filled bottle after bottle with wine. The noise? It was loud, but we were able to comfortably listen to our guide Bill Flint as he disclosed that their operation completed 8,000 cases a day. That's 96,000 bottles! Keep in mind that J. Lohr bottles year-round at two production facilities—all white wine is bottled in San Jose and all the reds in Paso Robles.

J. Lohr has two primary winemakers—Jeff Meier and Steve Peck. Steve joined the J. Lohr family in 2007 and oversees winemaking duties for all of their red wines. Jeff has been with the company since early 1984, when he worked his first harvest. Having a degree in enology and viticulture from the University of California at Davis, Jeff was offered a position as bottling line supervisor, then two years later he was promoted to assistant winemaker. In 1995, he became J. Lohr's director of winemaking.

FEATURED WINE: Cabernet Sauvignon, Chardonnay, Merlot and White Riesling
TASTING COST: Complimentary (up to six tastes)
HOURS: Daily, 10 AM-5 PM
LOCATION: 1000 Lenzen Avenue, San Jose
PHONE: 408-918-2160
WEBSITE: www.jlohr.com
GPS COORDINATES: 37.333966, -121.912825

San Martin

18 Clos LaChance Winery

Pulling onto Hummingbird Lane on our way to Clos LaChance Winery, we weren't sure what to expect. With vineyards to our right and rolling hills to our left, what lay around the next bend could be anyone's guess. After a mile's worth of wondering what was in store for us, we spied a very large wine production facility. Turning left per the signs and heading up the hill, we found ourselves in the parking lot of one of the most regal-looking wineries in all of Santa Clara County.

The winery's European architecture is stunning. Inside their elegant tasting room, Clos LaChance staff instantly greeted us. Knowing why we were there, one of them took us on a tour of the adjacent Grand Salon and then downstairs into the cellar room, available for private events, with its beautiful aged-looking stonework. Next we went upstairs to see a secret apartment for the owners and finally outside to witness the dramatic views from the Grand Veranda. It's hard to believe that the facility—which can be described simply as "old-world

elegance personified"—is not even ten years old.

Clos LaChance Winery actually is a home winemaker's hobby gone crazy. In 1987, Bill and Brenda Murphy planted a few rows of Chardonnay in their Saratoga backyard as landscape and for making wine for personal use. A few short years later, their wine was good enough to sell, and they did just that, releasing their first offering— a Chardonnay—in 1992. Four years later, the couple formed "CK Vines" (named after their two daughters Cheryl and Kristin), a vineyard maintenance and installation company specializing in backyard vineyard development.

At the time all of this was happening, Bill also was employed as the director of Internet marketing at Hewlett-Packard, a job he retired

from in 2000 after 30 years with the company. When asked about his "aha moment" as it relates to his passion for being a winery owner, Bill explained, "As our kids got out of high school, Brenda and I thought that running a business together would be the next stage of our lives. I would be getting out of high tech; she would have time with the kids gone. Given we had a backyard vineyard and an interest in growing grapes and making wine, we concluded that wine would be our future."

From their small backyard vineyard to their current 150 acres of vines and annual production of 60,000 cases, the Murphy's dream certainly has been realized, if not exceeded. Working side by side with them are their two daughters, Cheryl Murphy Durzy, who oversees all areas of sales and manages the company's brand, and Kristen Murphy, who is in charge of weddings and corporate events, CK Vines and other outside business ventures. "They bring energy, spark, drive and commitment, ensuring the success of our multigenerational wine business," Bill bragged, as any proud father would do. "We would like nothing more than to have the third generation join us as well. It may take a while—the oldest grandchild is six!"

How the winery got its moniker "Clos LaChance" is an interesting story. In French, "clos" translates to a small, enclosed, fenced-in vineyard, while "LaChance" is Brenda's maiden name. The hummingbird logo was chosen by the Murphys for both its beauty and ability to keep other birds away from the grapes. It's easy to see why birds would want to nibble on the winery's premium estate grapes, especially after Clos LaChance became certified as a sustainable winery and vineyard by the California Winegrowing Alliance. Tenets of such an accolade include a winery's commitment to using practices such as solar power, water recycling and green pest management. "We want to continue to

---

WINE MYTH "Wine gets better the older it gets." — *Bill Murphy*

---

put our all into our estate vineyard and make the wines the best they can possibly be," daughter Cheryl said.

Besides showcasing their wines in their tasting room, Clos La-Chance offers five different tasting tours. "We run the tours every Saturday and Sunday at 11 AM and 1 PM," Cheryl said. The VIP tour, at $25 per person, includes an extensive look at the production facility, barrel room with barrel tasting and demonstration vineyard, followed by a tasting of five finished wines back in the tasting room. Because the tour is so popular, Cheryl strongly suggests reservations.

But you don't need to book a tour to enjoy the ambiance of everything Clos LaChance. Take, for instance, tasting their elegant wines— upwards of thirty different offerings—over their remarkable wood and zinc-topped tasting bar. Outside on the Grand Veranda, you can watch golfers playing the 6th hole of the adjacent Corde Valle Resort and Golf Course, meander down to the winery's mulberry grove or take up a game of bocce ball. And keep an eye out for winery dog Amber. A Rhodesian Ridgeback, Amber's main duties include eating, sleeping and gnawing on her squeaky toys, but, most importantly we learned, guarding her owner's library wine stash!

FEATURED WINE: Chardonnay, Pinot Noir, Meritage and Cabernet Sauvignon
TASTING COST: $5-$7
HOURS: Daily, 11 AM-5 PM
LOCATION: 1 Hummingbird Lane, San Martin
PHONE: 408-686-1050
WEBSITE: www.clos.com
GPS COORDINATES: 37.073405, -121.6437

19 Cinnabar Winery

S aratoga's Cinnabar Winery, located on Big Basin Way between 5th and 6th Streets, is a gem of a tasting room. From its delectable wines to its child-friendly atmosphere to its knowledgeable and entertaining staff, this place is a must-stop during your wine tour.

Tom Mudd—Cinnabar's founder—enjoyed drinking Santa Cruz Mountain wines so much that he decided to try making some of his own wine under a home label. But before launching into a career as a winemaker and winery owner, Tom, who passed away in 2007, was more than a little busy. Born in the 1940s in Los Angeles, he learned about agriculture on his family's 360-acre Malibu Mountains ranch. After finishing high school, Tom headed to Stanford where he studied engineering and pre-med, earning a degree in 1964. Upon graduation, he traveled extensively and from 1969 to 1973 worked with the Sierra Club specializing on water issues. Afterward, he returned to Stanford

University where he earned a master's degree in environmental engineering and then a Ph.D. in civil engineering.

While working toward those two degrees, Tom attended a harvest party in Woodside where he became hooked on winemaking. He

planted a one-acre vineyard on his small property and took viticulture and enology classes at the University of California at Davis, in conjunction with his Stanford studies. Recognizing his love for wine, he went on a quest for more property to plant more grapes; no place other than the Santa Cruz Mountain region would do. He spent a year looking, even utilizing a helicopter to search for his ideal plot of land, and he found it on that trip—his 22-acre slice of paradise was perched on the eastern rim of the mountains, just above Saratoga. He planted his dream vineyard, using cuttings from vines with very rich DNA history from renowned French vineyards such as Chateau Margaux and Corton-Charlemagne. With the release of a Cabernet Sauvignon in 1986, Cinnabar Winery came to be.

One fun aspect of Tom's reverence for science can be found in the name of his winery. "Cinnabar" is loosely defined as a heavy reddish mercuric sulfide that is the principal ore of mercury. It is also commonly referred to as "vermilion." In the 14th century, medieval scientists called alchemists believed they could transform ordinary metals to gold through "alchemy," using the mineral cinnabar. Thus, the bright red or purple-red mineral became highly coveted. The comparison is wonderful, as the same can be said for taking grapes and turning them to liquid gold—Cinnabar wine.

When Tom passed away in 2007, the Saratoga estate was sold. But Tom's commitment to creating wine remains in the hands of Cinnabar president Suzanne Frontz and winemaker George Troquato, who joined the company in 1990. A third-generation winemaker, George worked side-by-side with Tom and loves complex and non-traditional wines as much as Tom did. Since the estate vineyard was sold, the company purchases their fruit from numerous growers throughout California, but that hasn't stopped George from creating great wines, now or in the future. "Mother Nature makes a different offering every year," George said, commenting on the existence of a winemaker, "but you only get 20 to 30 vintages in a lifetime."

As mentioned earlier, Cinnabar's tasting room is a joy. While tasting, wander around and examine an array of wine-related items, including "Baskets by Cinnabar," a line of gift items that pairs their wine with gourmet foods. Cinnabar also hosts a child-friendly environment, featuring a safe play area with agricultural-themed coloring books and crayons. The staff also gladly will offer their younger guests complimentary grape juice.

FEATURED WINE: Chardonnay, Pinot Noir, Malbec and Bordeaux blends
TASTING COST: $5, refunded with purchase
HOURS: Daily, 11 AM-5 PM; May-September, open until 7 PM on
Fridays and Saturdays
LOCATION: 14612 Big Basin Way, Saratoga
PHONE: 408-867-1012
WEBSITE: www.cinnabarwine.com
GPS COORDINATES: 37.255733, -122.036179

20 Cooper-Garrod Estate Vineyards

Cooper-Garrod Estate Vineyards, located in the foothills just outside of Saratoga, is the quintessential family agricultural operation. In business since 1893, it only took 100 years for the family to go commercial with their winery business.

A lot has happened over the course of those 100 years. The Garrod family homesteaded the land at the turn of the 20th century and planted prune and apricot orchards. Flash forward nearly 50 years. Louise Garrod married George Cooper in 1941 and shortly thereafter, George became a pilot and fought in WWII as a member of the 412th Fighter Squadron. After the war, George went on to enjoy a storied career as chief research test pilot for NASA. In 1973, he retired to the ranch with Louise and decided to plant vineyards, thinking it would be a fun hobby. His nephew—Jan Garrod—agreed, saying that grow-

The original 1922 fruit house serves as the estate's tasting room.

ing grapes would be a good continuation of the family's agricultural heritage. The vineyards loved the Santa Cruz Mountain terroir and the fruit became so well-regarded that the family sold grapes to wineries for years and made wine for personal use. It took the family another two decades to release wine commercially under the Cooper-Garrod label.

"Our 3,000 case annual production is entirely from estate San-

> **WINE MYTH** "Wine is made in the tank (opposed to in the vineyard)."
> *— Doris Cooper*

ta Cruz Mountains appellation fruit," said Doris Cooper. Married to George and Louise's son Bill—who is the winemaker—Doris is Cooper-Garrod's marketing director. "We've planted more vineyards since 1973 and have 28 acres in vines now . . . we are small and rustic, with no dreams of ever becoming an Italianate villa!" And how right she is, and in a good way. Here you will find no marble floors or columned arches, but instead you'll see a working horse ranch and stables, antique and modern farming equipment and buildings over 100 years old. It is hard to believe that such a rural setting is less than a half hour away from the urban heart of the Silicon Valley.

But let's get back to George: now in his 90s, he is at the winery every day, even after his son Bill, who apprenticed under his father, took over most of the winemaking duties. Having completed a successful career with the Foreign Service, and meeting his future wife Doris when she visited Warsaw, Bill returned to the ranch where he had grown up. He worked side-by-side with his dad, learning the craft of winemaking while taking extension classes from the University of California at Davis. With the move toward sustainable agriculture, Bill and Jan have taken Cooper-Garrod to the next step, getting their vineyards and winery certified by the California Certi-

fied Organic Farmers and the California Sustainable Winegrowing Alliance.

A visit to Cooper-Garrod Estate Vineyards and their tasting room is not to be missed. More than likely, you'll be served by a family member. Doris explained, "On special event days, you might meet all three generations who live and work here: our founding winemaker (3rd generation), his daughter or son (4th generation) and a grandchild (5th generation), all in the tasting room. When it's your name on the label, you might as well be the one pouring the wine!" Tasting is done in three flights: one complimentary (two wines) and two Proprietor's Flights (six or seven wines in a regular wine glass for $5 or in a 16-ounce souvenir glass for $10).

The tasting room is a treat in and of itself. The building is known as "The Fruit House"—it is here, 100 years ago, that the Garrod family stored their prunes and apricots before shipping the produce to market. "Grandma Garrod wanted a wooden floor so there could be community dances after the fruit was shipped, and there could be square dancers dancing around each of the three center posts, which are eucalyptus trunks hewn from the ridgeline atop our property," Doris pointed out. Those wooden posts are still in their original places, as is the wood floor. Also found inside is a fine collection of wine-related merchandise and kitchenware, as well as photos of George Cooper in his heyday as a WWII flying ace and research pilot for NASA.

One unique sidebar to this winery is that an active riding stable can be found onsite. Garrod Farms Riding Stables, established in 1960, offers guided one-hour trail rides. They probably prefer that you taste wine *after* your ride! To learn more, visit www.garrodfarms.com.

FEATURED WINE: Chardonnay, Viognier, Cabernet Franc and Cabernet Sauvignon
TASTING COST: Complimentary flight of two wines; $5-$10 for Proprietor's Flight
HOURS: Monday-Friday, 12 PM-5 PM; Saturday and Sunday, 11 AM-5 PM
LOCATION: 22645 Garrod Road, Saratoga
PHONE: 408-867-7116
WEBSITE: www.cgv.com
GPS COORDINATES: 37.276396, -122.05973

Saratoga

21 The Mountain Winery

The Mountain Winery—historically known as the Paul Masson Winery—is one of those places you don't want to miss. Their slogan is "Minutes Away, Worlds Apart," and we found this to be true, especially after driving up their one-mile-long access road. The 1,300-foot climb from the valley road to the top was at times a touch twisty, but the stunning view alone was worth it.

Most might know Mountain Winery as a premier destination for world-class entertainment. Their 2,500-seat outdoor venue hosts more than 70 concerts a year, including performances by Tony Bennett, Stevie Wonder and Melissa Etheridge. But many come for the wine, and well they should since this winery played an important role

in the development of California's agricultural heritage.

Over a century ago, Paul Masson planted his "Vineyard in the

Sky." Here's the short version: Masson arrived in San Francisco in 1878 from the Burgundy region of France. The son of winemakers, he knew the craft well, which led him to meet winery owner Charles LeFranc. At that time, LeFranc was married to Marie Adele Thée, whose father Éthienne Thée founded New Almaden Vineyard and Winery with LeFranc. In 1887, LeFranc was killed in an accident and the company passed to his three children, one of them being Louise who Paul Masson married a year later.

From 1888 on, Masson was busy carrying on the LeFranc wine name and dynasty, including making champagne under a new label— LeFranc Masson Wine Company. It wasn't until a very successful debut of their champagne during the Paris Expo of 1900 that the world started referring to the winery as "Paul Masson Champagne of California." Following this accolade, Masson built his own winery just outside of Saratoga on a mountain that literally touched the sky. His winery was completed in 1905, but the 1906 San Francisco earthquake damaged much of it. Undeterred, Masson rebuilt his winery, using a 12th century Spanish stone portal, taken from the earthquake rubble of San Jose's St. Patrick's Cathedral, for the winery's grand entrance. And here's a behind-the-scene's tidbit not many visitors know: the large inscription of the year "1852" over this famed Spanish portal marks the first year that Éthienne Thée—Louise's grandfather—planted Mission grapes in the New Almaden vineyard.

The years between the great earthquake and Prohibition were wonderful times for Masson and Louise. But by the time Prohibition was repealed in 1933, Masson was a widower and had lost most of his fortune. In 1936, he sold his beloved winery to Martin Ray. Ray thought highly of Masson and kept the Masson name intact. Masson passed away in 1943 at age 82.

Since then, the winery has changed hands many times, with the most current owners purchasing the property in 1999, replanting the historic vineyards in 2004 and 2009 and opening under the Mountain Winery label in 2009. Their winemaker is Jeffrey Patterson, founder and owner of Mount Eden Vineyards in Saratoga. (For a complete history, visit the winery's website.)

When visiting, be sure to walk down and view the outdoor concert venue, including the historic door that sits near the main stage. The home adjacent to the concert venue is perched overlooking the valley floor. It is called the "Chateau," and is the home where the Massons entertained presidents, movie stars and authors, according to Rhonda Boos, the winery's sommelier. "The building was preserved for its historical significance and used up until 2007 for concert dining," Rhonda explained. "Today, the building forms a beautiful backdrop for dining at the Chateau Deck Restaurant—our white tablecloth dining experience—and the Chateau Wine Bar, a great place to try a flight of our wines and enjoy the spectacular view off the Vista Deck."

The Mountain Winery's tasting room is transitory; because the property is so varied and large, it might be located anywhere on any given day. Besides the location Rhonda mentioned above, during the winter months the tasting room could be found in the historic winery's "Artist's Room" where guests can enjoy their wine and inspect concert memorabilia. Or during the warmer months, the tasting room might be outside on their expansive patio overlooking the property. And when you visit, ask if Jesse "The Mayor" Montenegro is on duty. The winery's official historian, he'll spellbind you with story after story about the mountaintop winery.

FEATURED WINE: Chardonnay and Pinot Noir
TASTING COST: $10-$18
HOURS: Friday-Sunday, 12 PM to 5 PM
LOCATION: 14831 Pierce Road, Saratoga
PHONE: 408-741-2822
WEBSITE: www.mountainwinery.com
GPS COORDINATES: 37.255789, -122.056479

Santa Clara County

More Area Wineries

Gilroy
Fortino Winery
LOCATION: 4525 Hecker Pass Hwy., Gilroy
PHONE: 408-842-3305
WEBSITE: www.fortinowinery.com

Rapazzini Winery
LOCATION: 4350 Monterey Hwy., Gilroy
PHONE: 800-842-6262
WEBSITE: www.rapazziniwinery.com

Morgan Hill
Morgan Hill Cellars
LOCATION: 1645 San Pedro Avenue, Morgan Hill
PHONE: 408-779-7389
WEBSITE: www.morganhillcellars.com

Saratoga
Savannah-Chanelle Vineyards
LOCATION: 23600 Congress Springs Road, Saratoga
PHONE: 408-741-2934
WEBSITE: www.savannahchanelle.com

Winery Notes

Winery Notes

Side Trips

Henry Coe State Park

The mountains southeast of San Jose are home to Henry Coe State Park. For thousands of years, this had been the land of the Ohlone and Northern Valley Yokut Indians before becoming cattle country's Pine Ridge Ranch. Settled by Henry Coe and his family in 1905, the land was worked as a cattle ranch until 1953. It was then that Henry's daughter Sada donated the 12,230-acre ranch to Santa Clara County. Five years later, the property became a state park.

Today, Henry Coe State Park is the biggest state park in Northern California. With 87,000 acres and 250 miles of trails, this is a place where you can truly get lost—literally if you aren't careful. Very little of this mountainous, oak-studded park is open to motor vehicles. That makes hiking, mountain biking and horseback riding the only way to see most of what's here.

A few of the historic ranch houses remain, including one converted to a visitor center. Throughout the park's rugged hills are the old ranch's dirt roads, cattle fences and stock ponds filled with fish. Park terrain is rugged and there is little drinking water available, so bring plenty of your own. This is a great backpacking park, with lots to see, including wildflowers and wildlife. If you desire a shorter hike, try the Monument Trail, which begins behind the old ranch house: the 1.2 mile loop trail takes you up to Pine Ridge and includes a stop at a memorial Sada built for her father (408-779-2728 or www.parks.ca.gov).

Hakone Gardens

Saratoga claims the Western Hemisphere's oldest Japanese residential garden where tranquility and serenity abound in this refuge of Asian-style solitude. Whether you visit to relax and enjoy the beautiful gardens, waterfalls and ponds or to learn more about Asian and Japanese culture, you won't be disappointed. More than 40,000 people visit each year and a third of those are foreign visitors from Asia, Europe and Australia.

Most visitors pass through the entry gates and spend an hour or two meandering along the garden's paths. These exquisite grounds were the setting for the garden scenes in the hit movie *Memoirs of a Geisha* (2005). If you have a little more time—and do a little pre-planning— you can arrange for a special tour or participate in a traditional Japanese tea ceremony. There are also classes ranging from Japanese watercolor and garden pruning to Tai Chi and Shiatsu Yoga. The small garden gift shop, which is also where you pay your entry fee, is filled with Asian delights from lamps to hand-carved granite lanterns (408-741-4994 or www.hakone.com).

Rosicrucian Egyptian Museum

This single-themed museum focuses on Egyptology, inside and out. The exterior design is reminiscent of the Temple of Amon at Karnak, and once inside, you'll wander through numerous galleries filled with the largest collection of Egyptian artifacts in western North America. There is a look at burial practices that includes vivid descriptions along with the tools used to prepare bodies for the afterlife, from liquefying and removing the brain to body mummification. Everyday items dating back a few thousand years include hair brushes, medicine bottles and even a jar thought to be for drinking beer; it has a rounded bottom so the imbiber couldn't put it down until he had drunk it dry!

The museum also has a planetarium—the Rosicrucian Planetarium—that features shows daily. Built in 1936, the planetarium is one of the oldest in the U.S. and the first to house an American-made star projector. Today, a newer projector is used and is capable of shifting the night sky forward or backward by 13,000 years. Outside is Rosicrucian Park, where you can wander through the Peace Garden (408-947-3635 or www.rosicrucianegyptianmuseum.org).

Intel Museum

At the Intel Museum, you'll find 10,000 square feet of exhibits that illustrate the technological developments of one of the nation's biggest and most successful tech companies. Even though the focus is on Intel's own technology, many of the exhibits are illustrative of computer-related manufacturing companies throughout the Silicon Valley. Some exhibits are hands-on, such as the unique opportunity to jump into a "bunny suit," those dust-free, ultra-clean coveralls that the manufacturing technicians wear. You can even write your name in binary code and get yourself "digitized" as you create a digital postcard (408-765-0503 or www.intel.com/about/companyinfo/museum/index.htm).

Gilroy Gardens

This is one place that you must see to believe. The park originally opened in 2001 as California's only horticultural theme park. Besides the gardens filled with trees, flowers, water elements and rock formations, it is also home to the famous Circus Trees. Each tree is different, such as the basket tree, which is actually 42 different sycamore trees grafted together to form a basket. The Circus Trees were originally "grown" by Axel Erlandson back in the 1940s and '50s. Other trees are shaped like hearts, lightning bolts, and even a four-legged giant. There are several different gardens within the park, as well as a water park and amusement rides (408-840-7100 or www.gilroy gardens.org).

Each of the Gilroy Gardens' 19 world famous Circus Trees has its own unique size, shape and beauty. (Photo courtesy of Gilroy Gardens)

Mt. Madonna County Park

If you're in the Hecker Pass area, you're in for a treat if you like outdoor adventure. This 3,688-acre park, with views of Santa Clara Valley to the east and Monterey Bay to the west, features redwood forests, oak woodlands and grassy meadows to explore. Equestrians and hikers can enjoy the 14-mile trail system; one trail leads to Henry Miller's summer home. Miller—the cattleman, not the writer—arrived with the Gold Rush and during his 70-year career, grew his fortune to $40 million by creating a California cattle and sheep industry that was second to none.

Camping is popular at Mt. Madonna County Park; the park has four campgrounds with 118 sites and 17 partial hook-up RV sites. The park also has an archery range and a visitor center that showcases the cultural and natural history of the region (408-842-2341 or www. sccgov.org/portal/site/parks/).

Winchester Mystery House

M uch like her home, Sara Winchester was a mystery. Money wasn't an issue when she began adding onto the unfinished eight-room farmhouse she purchased just outside San Jose in 1884. She was heir to the Winchester firearms company with an income of $1,000 per day, plus a few million in cash following her husband's death. Along with servants, she hired a team of carpenters and instructed them to begin adding on to her home—24 hours a day, seven days a week.

As they continued building, Sara would often change her mind and leave a partially-finished room unfinished with its doors leading to nowhere. Some doors would exit upper-story rooms into mid-air outside. She spent $9,000 on her ballroom in the days when people built entire houses for $1,000, but it went unused because she never invited guests into her home. And Sara immediately fired any of her well-paid employees if she heard them talking about her "craziness."

By the time Sara died in 1922, she had spent $5.5 million on her mansion that had grown to include 160 rooms. Today, the mansion is open for public tours that meander up strange stairways, down narrow hallways and through doors that don't always go where you might think they should. There is also an exhibit of antique Winchester firearms (408-247-2000 or www.winchestermysteryhouse.com).

For More Information

The Wineries of Santa Clara Valley
408-842-6436
www.santaclarawines.com

Santa Clara Convention & Visitors Bureau
1850 Warburton Avenue
Santa Clara, CA 95050
800-272-6822
www.santaclara.org

San Jose Convention and Visitors Bureau
408 Almaden Blvd.
San Jose, CA 95110
800-SAN-JOSE or 408-295-9600
www.sanjose.org

Santa Clara Chamber of Commerce
1850 Warburton Avenue
Santa Clara, CA 95050
408-244-8244
www.santaclarachamber.com

Gilroy Visitors Bureau
7780 Monterey Street
Gilroy, California 95020
408-842-6436
www.gilroyvisitor.org

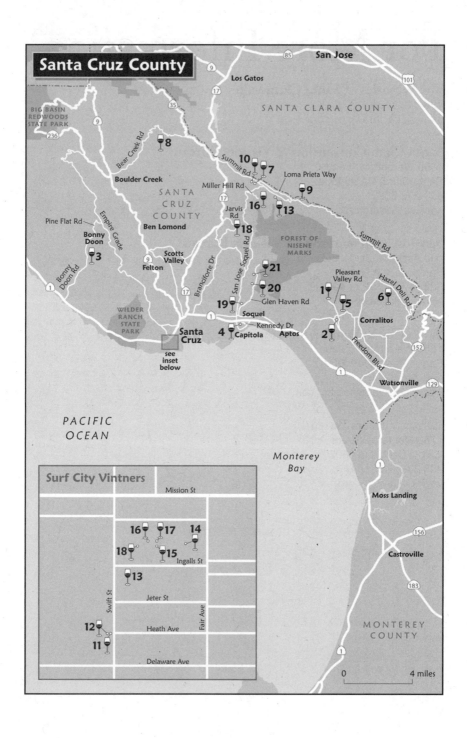

Santa Cruz County

San Jose

Los Gatos

SANTA CLARA COUNTY

BIG BASIN
REDWOODS
STATE PARK

8

Bear Creek Rd

Boulder Creek

Summit Rd

10 7

Loma Prieta Way

Miller Hill Rd

9

SANTA
CRUZ
COUNTY

Pine Flat Rd

Empire Grade

Ben Lomond

Jarvis
Rd

16 13

Bonny
Doon

3

Bonny Doon Rd

Scotts
Valley

Felton

18

San Jose Soquel Rd

FOREST OF
NISENE
MARKS

Summit Rd

Branciforte Dr

21

Pleasant
Valley Rd

Hazel Dell Rd

WILDER
RANCH
STATE
PARK

19

20

Glen Haven Rd

1

6

Soquel

5

Corralitos

Santa
Cruz

see
inset
below

4

Capitola

Kennedy Dr

Aptos

2

Freedom Blvd

152

Watsonville

129

PACIFIC
OCEAN

Monterey
Bay

1

Moss Landing

Surf City Vintners

Mission St

16

17

14

18

15

Ingalls St

13

Jeter St

Swift St

Fair Ave

12

Heath Ave

11

Delaware Ave

MONTEREY
COUNTY

Castroville

156

183

1

0   4 miles

Chapter Three

Since it is a mountainous wine appellation or AVA (American Viticultural Area) with many miles of narrow twisting roads, finding some of Santa Cruz County's wineries can be as much of an adventure as finding a great new wine. Old-fashioned paper maps are always a wise thing to bring on your Santa Cruz Mountains wine tasting adventures. But, you've got your trusty GPS! Right? Hmmm, well, on a couple of occasions ours had us going over back roads in miles-long circles, round and round. Yes, GPS units are great around the city of Santa Cruz and in many other areas, yet on some roads where mountains and trees interfere with the satellites, they can be more frustrating than useful.

And speaking of frustration, because county lines, AVAs and U.S. Postal Service delivery boundaries don't always match, you'll find a few wineries physically located in Santa Cruz County and part of the Santa Cruz Mountains AVA that have Santa Clara County addresses. This is especially true around Los Gatos.

For decades Santa Cruz has been known mostly for its great surfing and its boardwalk rollercoaster. Now, wine is regularly included in that list of popular attractions. There are more than 70 wineries in the Santa Cruz Mountains appellation. Although many wineries aren't open regularly for public tastings, there are more than enough to keep any wine lover busy tasting different offerings for weeks!

Wine is not a new commodity in the Santa Cruz Mountains though, as people have been making wine here for more than 150 years. In 1981, the Santa Cruz Mountains became one of the first federally recognized AVAs in the United States. Today, there certainly are numerous newcomers when it comes to Santa Cruz vineyards and winemakers, but with the county's excellent soils and the mild coastal-influenced weather, it's not difficult to understand why so many winemakers are making so much great wine.

When you aren't wine tasting, there's plenty of other things to see and do in Santa Cruz County besides the aforementioned surfing and rollercoaster riding. This is a very rural region, with an abundance of state and regional parks. From ocean beaches to giant redwoods to coastal scrub, there is something for everyone including hikers, equestrians, mountain bikers, campers and fishing enthusiasts. You can go hiking in California's oldest state park

The Santa Cruz Mountains rise behind the popular Santa Cruz Beach Boardwalk.

at Big Basin Redwoods, experience huge elephant seals in action at Año Nuevo or try mountain biking in The Forest of Nisene Marks State Park, the epicenter of the 1989 Loma Prieta earthquake. One of the state's biggest temblors, it registered 6.9 on the Richter scale, caused 63 deaths and resulted in $6 billion in damage. In comparison, the infamous 1906 San Francisco earthquake registered between 7.7 and 8.25. This earthquake and the raging fires that followed brought about an estimated 3,000 deaths and did $9.5 billion in damage (in today's dollars).

Aptos

1   Nicholson Vineyards

Marguerite and Brian Nicholson are the owners of Nicholson Vineyards. They opened their winery in June 2004 when they released two wines—estate-grown and bottled Chardonnay and Pinot Noir. "It had always been a dream of ours," Marguerite observed when asked why they opened a winery. "Do we enjoy the fruits of our labor? Yes, of course! We love our wine!"

Located in the Corralitos foothill region of the Santa Cruz Mountains, Nicholson Vineyards hosts four acres of Chardonnay and Pinot Noir grapes separated into three blocks. The vines were originally planted in 1996 and the Pinot Noir portion was expanded in 2004. While many Santa Cruz Mountain vineyards are perched in the hills,

the Nicholson's property is at an elevation of 700 feet; such a unique microclimate allows for an extended growing season. They produce more than 1,000 cases of wine annually, and besides their estate-grown offerings, they purchase grapes from local vineyards. Their winemaker is Ian Brand, who was the assistant winemaker and vineyard manager at Big Basin Vineyards (Santa Cruz) before joining Nicholson Vineyards in 2008. "He's an amazing young man who is passionate about the winemaking process. We learn something new from him every day," Marguerite said.

Besides their wines, Nicholson Vineyards produces estate olive oil. "It is extra virgin and cold pressed," Marguerite explained. "Our oil is available for sale at the winery each December and sells out within the month. It is very tasty!"

We always ask about the history of a winery or vineyard, but when we asked this time, we were in for a surprise. Brian is a ninth-generation Californian, a direct descendent of Felipe Santiago Garcia and his wife Petra Alcentera de Lugo. That's a statement few can make. Brian's family was among the first Spanish families to come to Alta California, traveling from Mexico to the Royal Presidio of San Diego in 1774 with an expedition led by Lt. Don Jose Francisco de Ortega. In November 1774, Petra gave birth to a baby boy they named Juan Jose Garcia. The oldest of 20 children born to the couple, Juan Jose was the first native son of

California born to Spanish parents. Father Junipero Serra confirmed Juan Jose at Mission San Carlos de Monterey in 1784.

During his career in the Spanish military, Felipe Santiago served at several California presidios including the Royal Presidio de Monterey. It is here where Petra died in 1817, and Felipe buried her at the Royal Presidio Chapel of San Carlos de Monterey. Felipe died five years later and was buried next to his wife.

When we visited, the Nicholsons had moved their tasting room outside, underneath the large overhang that covers the winery's entrance, to take advantage of the beautiful weather. With the winery right next to the vineyard, the olive orchard and stately oak trees, Nicholson Vineyards is a relaxing place to enjoy a picnic and glass of wine.

FEATURED WINE: Chardonnay, Pinot Noir, Syrah and Zinfandel
TASTING COST: $10
HOURS: Saturday, 12 PM-4 PM
LOCATION: 2800 Pleasant Valley Road, Aptos
PHONE: 831-724-7071
WEBSITE: www.nicholsonvineyards.com
GPS COORDINATES: 37.004483, -121.839731

2 Pleasant Valley Vineyards

Pulling into the driveway of Pleasant Valley Vineyards, we did not know what to expect. A small building sat to one side of the driveway and parking was at a minimum. (We discuss vehicle limitations at the close of this entry.) But at the top of the hill was a beautiful home. We parked and walked up. Just then, through a side gate, owner Cathy Handley greeted us. She led us into the backyard where we met her husband Craig, also an owner and their winemaker.

At this point, we were still looking for their tasting room. Walking up the stairs and onto their raised redwood deck, we came upon

a tasting bar. Considering that it was a beautiful day, it made sense to have it outside! But what surprised us was the view of the yard itself—it was beautiful! Perfectly manicured hillside vineyards ringed the bowl-shaped yard, the gardens were impeccable and a towering cathedral grove of redwoods stood majestically to one side. These "circle of trees" were once prevalent in this region, mainly near the town of Corralitos, only a five-minute drive away. Historians say that this may be how Corralitos came by its name: the trees created natural "corrals" for live-stock. But the only thing the Handleys had corralled was a well-used hammock!

Cathy and Craig planted their five-acres of estate Pinot Noir and

Chardonnay grapes in 1996, the same year they established their business. Both varietals are select French Dijon clones. We wanted to learn more, so Craig ex-plained, recounting that in the late 1970s, Raymond Bernard, a French viticulturist at the University of Dijon in Burgundy, France, took cuttings from select Burgun-dian vineyards. "This plant material came to be known, collec-tively, as the 'Dijon clones.'"

Besides Pinot Noir and Chardon-nay, the Handleys make other varietal wines, purchasing fruit from select vineyards in the state. The way they have named their wine is endearing; five are named for their grandchildren: Brittany Morgan Chardonnay; Dylan David Pinot Noir; Austin Craig Zinfandel; Casey

Alexander Merlot and Abby Madison Cabernet Sauvignon. Plus there are two wines named for a grandnephew and grandniece—Sean Boyle Syrah and Erika Anna Viognier.

Craig and Cathy became passionate about wine more than 40 years ago. "Cathy and I grew up just south of Napa and Sonoma, and we came of age in the mid-'60s. We enjoyed weekend outings, riding our bikes from Sonoma to Napa," Craig reflected, adding that the couple would buy a picnic lunch then ride to wineries in the region. "We

would meet and be greeted by the pioneers of the industry at Beringer, Mondovi, Inglenook, Cake Bread, Hetiz, Christian Brothers and many others."

The couple's appreciation for wine grew as a result of Craig's career selling mushrooms (no, not the 'shrooms from his "coming-of-age" days in the 1960s). Craig spent nearly four decades in the mushroom industry, selling and marketing fresh mushrooms and spawn—the starter culture equivalent to seed—around the world. During his travels, with Cathy joining him when possible, they had the unique opportunity to meet professional chefs, wine writers and foodies, as well as visit many of the best wine regions on the planet.

Vehicle limitations: parking is limited and there is no turnaround. Buses are not allowed—no exceptions—and all vans and limousines must make appointments beforehand.

FEATURED WINE: Pinot Noir, Chardonnay, Cabernet Sauvignon and Syrah
TASTING COST: $10-$15
HOURS: April-September, Saturday, 12 PM-4 PM; November-March, third Saturday, 12 PM-4 PM; October, closed
LOCATION: 600 Pleasant Valley Road, Aptos
PHONE: 831-288-0074
WEBSITE: www.pvvines.com
GPS COORDINATES: 36.983833, -121.827065

Bonny Doon

3 Beauregard Vineyards

In the Santa Cruz Mountains, the name "Beauregard" is synonymous with quality. The Beauregard family has been growing grapes in these mountains for more than 60 years. Through their hard work, determination and love of the land, four generations of Beauregard men have created some of the most well known vineyards in this region.

Amos Beauregard started the family grape growing business in 1949. A retired sheriff's deputy, Amos planted 13 acres of Pinot Noir, Chardonnay and Cabernet Sauvignon grapes on his ranch in Bonny Doon. Amos' son Emmit "Bud" Beauregard and grandson Jim helped him plant and tend to the vineyards when they weren't working at Bud's store—Shopper's Corner Grocery Store. At age 11, Bud got a job at the store, which was established in 1938, and purchased it when he

was 18. The Santa Cruz landmark is one of the last remaining mom-and-pop stores in the area today.

Amos passed away in the 1970s. Bud took over his father's vineyard, with young Jim at his side, growing grapes purely for the love of the family land. When Bud retired in 2002, Jim took over the vineyards with the help of oldest son Ryan, and the store, with help from younger son Andre.

Having practically grown up in the vineyard, Jim is now a trained viticulturalist. It is Jim who is responsible for establishing the Ben Lomond Mountain wine appellation. "It's been my life's passion to bring notoriety to a region I think is extremely unique in its terroir," Jim  said. "I have spent almost 40 years sharing my passion of the area as it relates to the grape-growing business." The appellation, established in 1987, encompasses 9,000 acres of vineyards in the Ben Lomond Mountain and Bonny Doon region. This microclimate lends itself to maritime attributes through its extreme proximity to the ocean and its high elevations. "It might take my whole lifetime to prove that we have the best growing area in the world, but I am willing to work on it until then," Jim asserted. Needless to say, Jim's contribution to the grape growing legacy in this region is vast. In a nutshell, he mainly focused on managing area vineyards in the 1970s and '80s and became a partner in a few local vineyards. Over these years, he continued selling grapes from the Beauregard Ranch vineyard as well.

As Jim worked, his son Ryan—the fourth Beauregard man to become involved in the world of wine—paid close attention. Having played in his grandfather Bud's vineyards as a child, he remembers the family making wine in the old barn and learned from his father how to tend to the vineyard. Fast forward to Ryan in his 20s, working at different wineries in order to learn the craft from experienced winemakers and making his first wine—a Chardonnay—in 1998. A year later, father and son decided that since they were growing and selling some of the best grapes in the state, it was time to make their own family wine, and Beauregard Vineyards was born. They still source grapes to other wineries, but with Ryan's goal of growing the business to 10,000 cases annually using only Beauregard grapes—including grapes from his great grandfather's original 13 acres—the family hopes to grow into their crop within the next five years.

> **WINE MYTH** "All sweet wines are dessert wines and pair well with chocolate." — *Ryan Beauregard*

History is prevalent throughout this story and it holds true for Beauregard's tasting room, as well. Originally erected as a general store in the beginning of the 20th century, in 1950, the store transformed into the notorious Lost Weekend bar, famous for being run by Gary Dahl, creator of the Pet Rock phenomenon of the 1970s. In 1983, Randall Graham purchased the property and established Bonny Doon Vineyard. The building served as his tasting room until 2008 when he moved his business to Surf City Vintners. Up until that point, Beauregard Vineyards had their tasting room at the Santa Cruz Wharf, but in 2008, they purchased the historic property and relocated their winery operation and tasting room.

We fell in love with Beauregard Vineyards. Before going inside, we took a quick walk around and saw redwoods, a creek, gardens and lawn area, wooden picnic tables on the back deck, whimsical bird houses and even chickens. Inside, we were awed by the sheer size of the tasting room, which is rustic and fun in nature. You can tell that history has graced this place for generations. If only the walls could talk! We had a great time chatting with Beauregard staffers, who were extremely knowledgeable about their wine and the family history. Later we learned that many of the staff are sommeliers, cheese educators and even assistant winemakers. And speaking of winemakers, don't be surprised to find Ryan and his wife Rachel, who oversees the administrative side of the business, behind the bar offering you a taste of some of the best wine in the region.

FEATURED WINE: Chardonnay, Pinot Noir, Cabernet Sauvignon and Zinfandel
TASTING COST: $5, refunded with purchase
HOURS: Daily, 11 AM-5 PM
LOCATION: 10 Pine Flat Road, Bonny Doon
PHONE: 831-425-7777
WEBSITE: www.beauregardvineyards.com
GPS COORDINATES: 37.04205, -122.150502

4 Pelican Ranch Winery

Phil Crews knows a thing or two about science. A professor of chemistry and biochemistry at the University of California at Santa Cruz since 1970, Phil applied his science background when making his first batch of wine. His wife Peggy picks up the story from there: "Phil started making wine in the mid-1970s, beginning with banana wine! He quickly learned that in order to produce wine worth drinking he

needed to start with good fruit. Lucky for him, there was a grape glut in the late '70s and really high quality vineyards were willing to sell to home winemakers. By the time we met in 1980, winemaking was pretty much a condition of our marriage!"

Pelican Ranch Winery opened in 1997, and their first tasting room opened in 2003. Specializing in Rhone- and Burgundy-style wines, the Crews' buy only the best grapes from local vineyards, labeling their wines per the single-vineyard designation. Production is limited to 100 cases from each vineyard. When asked about a particular wine, Peggy said that tasting their Chardonnay is a must. "Even if you don't like Chardonnay, you need to try one of Phil's," Peggy suggested. "The distinctive characteristics of different growing regions really shine through in Phil's Chardonnays. Carneros Chardonnay is soft, Dry Creek Chardonnay has a citrus quality and Santa Cruz Mountain Chardonnay has a distinctive mineral quality."

Besides teaching chemistry and running a world-class marine research program at the university, Phil also teaches a class entitled "Introduction to Wines and Wine Chemistry" at the school. "This was a course I developed to teach chemistry to non-science majors. The 5-unit course is academically rigorous, which comes as a surprise to some students," Phil explained, noting he came up with the idea for the class after becoming a winemaker. "In addition to the science, we have guest speakers who lecture on topics such as wine and health and wines of Burgundy."

Phil carries over some of his teachings into their tasting room, with the goal to have everyone who visits learn something new about wine. For instance, Phil said that visitors should not make assumptions about a particular varietal until they have tried wines from several AVAs. "Pinot Noir from the Santa Cruz Mountains is a different critter than Pinot Noir from Napa," Phil cited as an example.

Phil at his other job.
(Photo courtesy of Steve Clabeausch)

The aforementioned reference to Phil's marine research program revolves around marine sponges. A noted expert in the field, Phil says his goal in life is to combine his love of winemaking and his university work with sponges. Co-mingling those two loves has created many memorable stories, and Peggy shared one: "Once, while conducting field work in the South Pacific, Phil needed to get 10 gallons of a chemical solvent from American Samoa to Tonga. The pilots of the Tonga Air flight were reluctant to transport this cargo, but changed their minds when offered two bottles of Pelican Ranch wine in exchange!"

While Phil oversees the winemaking duties at Pelican Ranch (and continues his professorship at the university), Peggy is in charge of the day-to-day management of the winery. "Like Phil, I continue my day job," Peggy said, who is a speech pathologist at a local hospital. "Both of us are used to working 50- to 60-hour weeks and, for the most part, thrive on it. It helps that we have flexible schedules and a home office. But it's an ongoing challenge to talk about non-winery subjects," she concluded, when asked about running a business together.

When trying to come up with a name for their winery, the Crews desired a moniker that would represent their love for living and working near the coast. It also had to sound "unpretentious and fun," Peggy said. Thus, they settled on Pelican Ranch Winery. "Just picture us herding them thar' pelicans on our ranch!" Peggy quipped.

In the beginning of 2011, the Crews moved their tasting room from Surf City Vintners to Capitola. Winding through a residential neighborhood, you'll find the tasting room in a small business complex at the very end of Kennedy Drive.

FEATURED WINE: Chardonnay, Pinot Noir, Pinotage and Viognier
TASTING COST: $5, waived with purchase
HOURS: Friday-Sunday, 12 PM-5 PM
LOCATION: 100 Kennedy Drive, #102, Capitola
PHONE: 831-426-6911
WEBSITE: www.pelicanranch.com
GPS COORDINATES: 36.983388, -121.94928

5 Alfaro Family Vineyards & Winery

Richard and Mary Kay Alfaro have the 1989 Loma Prieta earthquake to thank for pushing them into the wine business. The quake's epicenter was in The Forest of Nisene Marks State Park, only 10 miles northeast of the town of Santa Cruz. Registering 6.9 on the Richter scale, the quake did irreversible damage to life and property.

At the time of the quake, Richard and Mary Kay owned Alfaro's Micro Bakery in Santa Cruz. A unique bakery that made artisan breads, they had been open for only 14 months. Downtown Santa Cruz was their primary retail customer base, but the earthquake impacted their business tremendously, so much so they closed down and focused all

of their energy on selling their bread wholesale. This switch proved so successful that nine years later, the Sara Lee Corporation made them an offer they couldn't refuse. They sold the business and soon pursued their lifelong dreams of owning a winery.

The Alfaros, who both have extensive backgrounds in the food industry, had always been wine enthusiasts. They purchased a 100-year-old ranch in Corralitos and planted their first vineyard, naming it "Lindsay Paige Vineyard" after their daughter. They also planted a vineyard in their son Ryan Spencer's name. Over the years, more vineyards have been added, bringing their total to 38 acres, and in 2010, the Alfaros were certified by the California Certified Organic Farmers as organic grape growers.

We had a ball talking with both Mary Kay and Richard during our visit. We learned that Mary Kay oversees all of the administrative duties, including the tasting room and wine club. She is also a certified sommelier. "The sommelier certification was a great way to take my learning up a notch and taste wines outside the norm," Mary Ann said, adding that she is now better versed to talk about wine with tasting room guests. Richard is the outside sales person, grape grower and a self-taught winemaker. When asked about any similarities and/or differences he has found

Richard Alfaro in his barrel room

between making bread and making wine, Richard replied, "There are similarities between bread baking and winemaking—both use indigenous yeasts and are done on a small scale and both employ the science of fermentation, though one involves grains, the other, grapes."

> **WINE MYTH** "Pair white wine with chicken and fish, red wine with meat."
> *— Richard Alfaro*

Richard has done well with his winemaking: In February 2008, *Wine & Spirits Magazine* showcased Alfaro's 2005 Estate Syrah in an issue titled "Year's Best Syrah—94 Greats from Around the World." Mary Ann explained that over the course of learning the craft of wine-making, Richard realized that the old adage, "You can't make a silk purse out of a sow's ear," is true. "You need high quality grapes to make a great wine," they concluded. To learn more about the Alfaros, read their interview at **www.WineWherever.com**.

Alfaro's wine offerings are many, including a strong nod to one of Richard's favorites—Pinot Noir. What caught our eye was the beautifully painted family portrait hanging on the wall behind the tasting bar. It shows the Alfaro family in the vineyards, with Ryan standing in the bed of an old blue pick-up truck, Lindsay standing nearby and Mary Kay and Richard in mid-hug. But Richard has a puzzled look and is scratching his head. "Richard has a great sense of humor but also knows how much work it is to own a small business," Mary Kay said, noting that Santa Cruz artist Laurie Zeszut created the harvest-scene painting. "Laurie's depiction of him scratching his head is like him saying, 'Oh, no, here we go again! But let's have some fun with this!'" The painting is also used as a label for many of their wines.

Getting to Alfaro Family Vineyards and Winery was a little confusing since we didn't have our GPS with us, but relied instead on looking for street numbers. That was our mistake; we learned that street numbers in the Santa Cruz Mountains have no rhyme or reason. It's best to use the GPS coordinates below or print out directions found on the winery's website.

FEATURED WINE: Pinot Noir, Chardonnay, Merlot and Syrah
TASTING COST: $10
HOURS: Saturday, 12 PM-5 PM
LOCATION: 420 Hames Road, Corralitos
PHONE: 831-728-5172
WEBSITE: www.alfarowine.com
GPS COORDINATES: 36.991927, -121.819963

6   Windy Oaks Estate and Vineyard

Windy Oaks Estate and Vineyard owners Jim and Judy Schultze have lived in many parts of the world. It was while the Chicago-based couple, along with their two very young sons, were living in Australia in the late 1980s that Jim, an international management consultant, began studying wine as a hobby. He was fascinated by the concept—typical in Australia and Europe—of grape growing and winemaking being one continual process, and took it upon himself to learn everything he could about wine, including vineyard manage-

ment. In 1992, the family moved to London for Jim's work and spent long weekends traipsing through the winegrowing regions of Europe, including France, Italy and Spain.

In 1994, the Schultze family returned to the U.S. and settled

in Corralitos. A year later, adjacent property went up for sale. With all of his hands-on experience, coupled with classes in enology and viticulture taken at the University of California at Davis, Jim knew this would be a great opportunity to start their own vineyard. After purchasing the property, the Schultze family planted their first three acres of Pinot Noir in 1996. Today, they have a total of 18 acres planted to Pinot Noir and one acre planted in Chardonnay, all part of their estate vineyard. Their tasting room opened in 2005. Their oldest son James came up with the winery's name. "Our vineyard ridge has three old oak trees and it is often windy up there, which means that the vines have very good air flow," said Judy, adding James was only 16 years old at the time.

The Schultze's produce and offer for tasting and sale two varietals—Pinot Noir and Chardonnay. Both estate wines, they are made in the classic Burgundian style, referring to the Burgundy region of France where the Pinot Noir grape originated. "A Burgundian-style Pinot Noir usually means that the wine is more layered, more elegant, and less of a 'fruit bomb' than a more typical California Pinot Noir," Judy explained. "As such, the Burgundian style pairs well with many different foods." While their Pinot Noir is sensuous and full-bodied, their Chardonnay, Judy claimed, "is crisp with citrus flavors and a silky balanced finish, like a very good white Burgundy."

WINE MYTH "There is some special requirement that a person needs to enjoy wine." — *Judith Schultz*

When we visited Windy Oaks, we had the pleasure of meeting Spencer, the Schultze's younger son. He was very helpful and quite knowledgeable about wine. While both James and Spencer are involved in the family business, it is Spencer who is following in his father's footsteps, taking the Winemaker Certificate program at the University of California at Davis.

In addition to being open to the public on Saturday afternoons, Windy Oaks offers private, guided walking tours of their vineyard that include wine tasting and food. The costs starts at $25 per person for the full tour, wine tasting and light snacks, and can be upgraded to $35 per person for a gourmet box lunch on the vineyard's ridge overlooking Monterey Bay. Advance reservations are required.

FEATURED WINE: Pinot Noir and Chardonnay
TASTING COST: $10, refundable with $50+ purchase
HOURS: April through October; Saturdays, 12 PM-5 PM
LOCATION: 550 Hazel Dell Road, Corralitos
PHONE: 831-786-9463
WEBSITE: www.windyoaksestate.com
GPS COORDINATES: 37.019457, -121.759447

Los Gatos

7 Burrell School Vineyards & Winery

According to the folks at Burrell School Vineyards & Winery, you must promise to sip your wine. We're not kidding! The winery—located on the grounds where a historic 1890s' schoolhouse stands proudly today—has creatively used an elementary school-themed marketing approach for their business. As their saying goes, "School has never been this much fun!"

The 120-year-old Burrell Schoolhouse had served several functions over its many years, including being a one-room schoolhouse from 1890 to 1954, followed by a community center until its abandonment in 1966. It wasn't until 1973 that Anne and Dave Moulton purchased the property and began to plant

Historic schoolhouse adjacent to the tasting room

vineyards. They also spent more than twenty years restoring the school-house, which serves as their home. "The schoolhouse is the center point of our business," Dave said, "and it is the focus of our label and winery

theme." Nearly everything at Burrell School Winery is reminiscent of the "olden days" of blackboards and chalk. Their wine labels themselves are entertaining and whimsical, including Pinot Noir "Principal's Choice," Chardonnay "Teacher's Pet," Syrah "Spring Break" and Zinfandel "Detention Red."

Besides being the winery's owners, the Moultons each add their distinct touch to the place. Anne is the marketing genius and Dave, the winemaker. An electrical engineer working in the Silicon Valley, Dave began making wine at home in 1967. He attended enology and viticulture seminars at the University of California at Davis for more than twenty years, turning "pro"—as he terms it—in 1994. The winery's first release was in 1995.

The Moultons grow several estate varietals on their property: Chardonnay, Pinot Noir, Merlot, Cabernet Franc, Syrah, Cabernet Sauvignon and Petit Verdot. For their exclusive "Valedictorian" blend, they source grapes from the nearby Pichon Vineyard. They also purchase fruit from other local growers when needed. When we asked Dave for his favorite aspect of being a winemaker, he answered: "Each year we get a new crush and start the product chain all over, again and again."

Burrell School's vineyards sit at an elevation of 1,600 feet above sea level. Nearby Monterey Bay brings cool nights, perfect for the slow ripening of these cool-climate grapes. Pruning of the vines and harvesting of the fruit is all done by hand, with the goal, according to Dave, of nurturing the grapes in order to produce distinctive, concentrated wines reflective of their mountain home. For other vineyard duties, eight heritage Cletrac tractors are used. "The tractors were manufac-

> **WINE MYTH** "We sit around and drink wine all day." — *Anne Moulton*

tured for hillside vineyards between 1932 and 1954," Dave explained. "They are crawler type or 'track-layer' tractors." To learn more about Anne and Dave, read their interview at **www.WineWherever.com.**

Family plays an important role at Burrell School. The Moultons' two daughters have grown up at the schoolhouse and now as adults are involved in the business. The oldest is Elena Nelson, who manages the financial side of the winery, as well as overseeing their huge wine club. Younger daughter Marianne Martin is the president of their family corporation and, according to Anne, will be "the winemaker of the future."

Burrell School's tasting room opened in 1995. Located on the former site of the school's carriage house, which sits next door to the schoolhouse, the tasting room is absolutely darling. Inside we found many fun school-related references and items, including an old chalkboard with wines listed and a guest book inviting you to scribble comments with colored pencils. Each wine on the tasting menu had its own slate board in front of it with the name and year written out in chalk. On the outside veranda, you can enjoy sweeping vistas of the western slopes of Pine Flat Ridge. This picnic seating area is so popular that reservations must be made with staff and are limited to an hour or less.

FEATURED WINE: Pinot Noir, Cabernet Franc, Merlot and Syrah
TASTING COST: $5
HOURS: Thursday-Sunday, 11 AM-5 PM
LOCATION: 24060 Summit Road, Los Gatos
PHONE: 408-353-6290
WEBSITE: www.burrellschool.com
GPS COORDINATES: 37.122249, -121.93239

| 8 | Byington Winery & Vineyards

When Idaho farm boy Bill Byington left the family farm in the 1940s and headed to California, it's a safe bet that he hadn't planned on becoming a prominent winery owner in the Santa Cruz Mountains more than 40 years later.

(Photo courtesy of Byington Winery)

After serving in WWII, Bill attended college where he learned the art of heat-treating, a process of using heat to alter the physical properties of a material. With his newfound knowledge and a mere $800 in hand, Bill established Byington Steel in Santa Clara. It was 1950 and this forward-thinking entrepreneur was only 26 years old. Today, the company is the largest of its kind in Northern California.

Back in the late 1950s, Bill and his

wife Mary purchased 95 acres of prime Santa Cruz Mountain land. Thirty years later, Bill's neighbor David Bruce—owner of David Bruce Winery in Los Gatos—told him he should consider planting Pinot Noir grapes on his property. Very fond of wine, the Idaho farm boy did just that and Byington Winery & Vineyard became a reality in 1989.

Now in his 80s, Bill no longer plays an active role in the winery. But the family is still in charge, with Bill's daughter-in-law Kathryn Byington in the role of CEO of this very successful wine estate. The day we visited, the place was alive with activity, from a bustling tasting room and many happy wine tasters to a festive family celebration taking place out on the expansive picnic grounds.

(Photo courtesy of Byington Winery)

Byington's winemaker is Andrew Brenkwitz. A native of Santa Cruz, Andrew graduated from California Polytechnic State University in San Luis Obispo with degrees in fruit science, viticulture and enology. While in college, Andrew worked part time at numerous wineries, including San Luis Obispo county favorites Wild Horse Winery and Vineyards and Justin Winery. He joined Byington in 2001, working under winemaker Don Blackburn and others until he became the primary winemaker eight years later. Andrew's self-described winemaking style is "old world with a modern flair" and his winemaking philosophy is to "keep the vineyard in the bottle." He has been known to take risks, which stems from his belief that there is "more than one way to do things when making wine."

Andrews's risks have paid off handsomely: Byington is known for two very unique blended wines. First is "Liage," a blend of Sauvignon Blanc and Viognier, and the second is a Bordeaux blend by the name of "Alliage." Each year, the wine is crafted using varietals such as Cabernet Sauvignon, Cabernet Franc and Merlot. It's important to note that Alliage is Bill Byington's favorite wine!

When tasting at Byington, be sure to wander outside and take in their impressive grounds. The picnic facilities include cloth-covered round tables with chairs and umbrellas and gas and charcoal grills (but you need to bring the cooking tools, et al). There's even a bocce ball court. The one thing not to miss is Byington's wine cave. Completed in 2002, the man-made cave sits 40 feet below their Pinot Noir vineyard and is available for special events. The winery also offers 45-minute educational (and entertaining) tours through their vineyard, production facility and wine cave. Of course you'll be treated to some wonderful wine, too! Reservations are required and there is a minimal per-person charge.

FEATURED WINE: Pinot Noir, Cabernet Sauvignon, Chardonnay and Sauvignon Blanc
TASTING COST: $5 refundable with purchase
HOURS: Daily, 11 AM-5 PM
LOCATION: 21850 Bear Creek Road, Los Gatos
PHONE: 408-354-1111
WEBSITE: www.byington.com
GPS COORDINATES: 37.170247, -122.052596

Los Gatos

9   Loma Prieta Winery

When we visited Loma Prieta Winery, we found it near the top of Santa Cruz's most notorious peak—Loma Prieta Mountain. The winery's slogan—"In the shadow of Loma Prieta"—is apropos because just a half mile away, a magnitude 6.9 earthquake struck and shook the San Francisco region to its core, literally. The date was October 17, 1989.

Laura Ness, marketing consultant for winery owners Paul and Amy Kemp, reported that living so close to the San Andreas Fault is not too worrisome for the Kemps. "It bothers everyone to the extent that it runs through some of the most populous portions of the state, but also some of the most remote."

On the upside of living so near to one of the most active fault

lines in the world, the Kemp's view, and that from the tasting room, is amazing. "We have one of the highest elevation vineyards and wineries in the Santa Cruz Mountains," Laura said, noting the 2,300-foot elevation. "The sweeping views of the entire Monterey Bay and coastline create a dramatic setting for relaxing and enjoying our excellent wines and special hospitality."

WINE MYTH "Red wines contain more sulfites than white wines."
— Amy Kemp

The Kemps opened their winery in 2003 when Paul, a personal injury attorney who continues to practice in the San Jose area, decided to take his winemaking hobby and turn it into a full-fledged enterprise. His first release that year was a Cabernet Sauvignon. Today, the couple has a three-acre vineyard on their property planted in Pinot Noir and a little grown varietal called Pinotage. A hybrid red grape from South Africa, Pinotage is starting to gain favor with wine lovers. According to Laura, Loma Prieta Winery is the only winery in the Santa Cruz Mountains to grow this varietal.

When you arrive at Loma Prieta's tasting room, be sure to go to the building to your right; the one to the left is the Kemp's residence. Inside, you'll find a beautiful tasting room and staff eager to pour you a taste of their wine. For fun, be sure to ask them the story behind "Deerly Departed," the name given to the deer head mounted over the fireplace. Depending on when you visit, this mascot will be festively decorated for the holiday or season at hand.

Outside, you'll find an expansive Italian-influenced patio with stone tables and benches, a bubbling fountain, a bocce ball court and a double-sided fireplace that is perfect if you're wine tasting on chilly days. And watch for Moe, the family's German Shorthair Pointer, who will probably hit you up for a game of ball!

FEATURED WINE: Pinot Noir, Cabernet, Viognier and Pinotage
TASTING COST: $5
HOURS: Saturday and Sunday, 12 PM-5 PM
LOCATION: 26985 Loma Prieta Way, Los Gatos
PHONE: 408-353-2950
WEBSITE: www.lomaprietawinery.com
GPS COORDINATES: 37.105078, -121.880667

Los Gatos

10 Regale Winery

Regale Winery concentrates on making "table-conscious" wines, in reverence to their philosophy that wine is inseparable from food. Their old-world ideals when it comes to food and wine pairings is the theme of their winery, ideals that are sure to please your palate and excite your senses.

Ashley DuBois, general manager and assistant winemaker at Regale, welcomed us. She and many of the staff were in the covered back patio, where a beautiful Italian-inspired tasting room was in place with a large wood-fired brick oven. The patio opened up to one of the most formal gardens we had seen on our journey through the Santa Cruz Mountains. It included fountains, bench walls, brick walkways, a spiral herb garden, a bocce ball court, outdoor fireplaces, mature olive trees and several quiet seating areas. "We want our visitors to give equal attention to our wines, our food offerings and our atmosphere. When

they leave and talk about Regale with friends, we want them to have a story worth sharing. Pizza tastings, bocce ball, estate olive oil tastings, amazing wines, complimentary tours of the winery and facilities, great conversation with our staff—all of these are of equal importance to us," Ashley explained.

It was then that owner and winemaker Larry Schaadt appeared. He picked up the tour from there, taking us upstairs to the winery's culinary kitchen and private dining room. We learned that Larry was once a real estate developer, but enjoyed wine so much that in the early 1990s he took winemaking extension classes from the University of California at Davis. With his newfound knowledge, Larry opened a private family-owned winery in Carmel Valley. Reared in the Los Gatos area, he always wanted to return home and start a winery here. "I wanted to do something close to town, but with a country setting. I wanted it to be a wine-country experience," Larry said. He bought the property a few days after it went on the market in 2006. "I lucked out and was driving by when I saw it." The property was destroyed in the 1989 Loma Prieta earthquake and the previous owners hadn't done much to revitalize it; Larry and his crew had their hands full turning the property into the Italian masterpiece it is today.

Regale's owner and winemaker Larry Schaadt

Standing in their state-of-the-art kitchen, Larry described the many facets of their multi-cultural culinary program. Under the watchful eye of winery chef Bruce Finch, students learn how to prepare a full meal from a chosen region of the world. Once completed, the students dine together in the winery's formal dining room, drinking, of course, Regale's estate-grown wine. Larry divulged that their most popular culinary classes focus on Italian, Mediterranean and French provincial cooking.

Regale offers complimentary food tastings to include fresh-baked bread and pizzas and their estate olive oils. "We press our own olive oil from our Tuscan trees, which are 17-year-old Saviano trees we had brought in and planted. That one Mission olive," Larry said, pointing out of a second-story window to the formal gardens below, "was the only one standing when we took over the property. It's a grand old tree, but we don't use it for any of our production."

Wine is a must when "food tasting" and visitors to Regale are treated to a flight of their premium wines for $10 per person, which includes their signature Pinot Noir from the Russian River Valley and their Alexander Valley Cabernet Sauvignon.

Regale Winery and Vineyards is just that—very regal. They know how to entertain and do so most lavishly with both food and drink. For this reason, they stress they are an adult environment and have no play areas for children. Also note that dogs are not allowed in the wine tasting area or the garden.

FEATURED WINE: Chardonnay, Pinot Noir, Cabernet Franc and Cabernet Sauvignon
TASTING COST: $10
HOURS: Saturday and Sunday, 12 PM-5 PM
LOCATION: 24040 Summit Road, Los Gatos
PHONE: 408-353-2500
WEBSITE: www.regalewine.com
GPS COORDINATES: 37.122835, -121.93327

11 Copious Winery

F or a change of pace when it comes to the wineries of Santa Cruz, be sure to stop by Copious Winery. This funky urban winery is daring, fun and supports and showcases local artists. They also focus on hospitality so when you visit, you are guaranteed to see one of the owners—Brandie or Lance Campbell. And if they have a babysitter, you'll see both!

The Campbells are new to Santa Cruz, but the couple and their wines are well regarded in the California Sierra foothills. The prior owners of Mount Aukum Winery, in the town by the same name, their reputation for terrific wines and great hospitality was second to none. It was during their time at Mount Aukum Winery the Campbells won more than 300 awards for their wines, internationally as well as in California, including Best of Class in both the *San Francisco Chronicle* and California State Fair annual competitions.

The Campbells favored the Santa Cruz area for family vacations, especially because of Lance's penchant for surfing, so when it was time for a change, they packed up and headed here. Copious Winery opened in 2010. They purchase all of their grapes, selecting product from only the finest vineyards in the state.

Originally from Texas, Lance worked as an artist in New Orleans before moving to San Francisco in 1996. There he worked as a bartender while attending the California School of Fine Arts. But he always had a passion for wine—his parents were avid collectors of rare bottles of Bordeaux wines. "Lance's parents traveled often and he knew where the key to the cellar was hidden. You can imagine what happened next!" Brandie said. Being in such close proximity to Napa, Lance gravitated in that direction and in 2000 he took a cellar job at Chateau St. Jean where he learned the craft of winemaking. He also studied at Seghesio Winery in Healdsburg. Known for their bold Zinfandels, it is here where, as Brandie put it, Lance "learned the art of Zin."

This urban winery is unpretentious and enjoyable. When we visited, we were mesmerized by the artwork, and especially tickled by the Copious tasting bar. Beneath a pane of glass on top of the bar were coins, and lots of them. Of course we had to ask, and Brandie explained. "When I met Lance, he was an artist and bartender in Austin, Texas. One of the most noticeable things in his apartment was a coffee table of coins he and some friends made when he lived in New Orleans," she said, noting they wanted to do the same thing for Copious. "We designed it ourselves and used most of the money from our three kids' piggy banks." Not to worry—the Campbells paid their kids back with cash.

Besides the artist aspect of Copious, it's their hospitality that makes them such a unique winery, for both their customers and especially their wine club members. Perks for members include occasional Friday night lounge parties with the winemaker or even hot-tubbing in their on-site, private spa room. The latter includes a complimentary glass of Copious wine and an appetizer.

Located just a few blocks from the Surf City Vintners' concentration of wineries, Copious can be found in a metal warehouse. The building is a multi-use facility and has many clients; watch for the winery's signage.

FEATURED WINE: Chardonnay, Cabernet Sauvignon and Pinot Noir
TASTING COST: $5, waived with purchase
HOURS: Friday-Sunday, 12 PM-5 PM
LOCATION: 427-A Swift Street, Santa Cruz
PHONE: 408-425-9463
WEBSITE: www.copiouswinery.com
GPS COORDINATES: 36.956558, -122.04882

Santa Cruz

12 Equinox

Equinox is the Santa Cruz Mountain's only sparkling wine producer open to the public. Located in west Santa Cruz, just a few blocks from Surf City Vintners, a stop at Equinox is a must, especially if you like the bubbly.

Owner and winemaker Barry Jackson, along with "Mrs. Winemaker" Jennifer Jackson, established Equinox in 1989 and opened their tasting room in 2007. Having no vineyards of their own, the Jacksons hand select their Chardonnay and Pinot Noir grapes from premium Santa Cruz Mountain vineyards. Besides their Equinox label of sparkling wines made in the tradition of "Méthode Champenoise," they have another label—Bartolo Wines. Recent releases included varietals such as Merlot and Syrah, as well as both a Bordeaux blend and a Mediterranean blend. Both labels are produced in very limited quantities.

The day we visited Equinox, Barry was thrilled to see us. Barry—now in his fifty-somethings—started making bootleg Applejack in high school because he couldn't buy beer. Since that time, he has worked in almost every aspect of the wine business: "Vineyards, wine production, equipment sales, built wineries, torn down wineries," Barry listed, adding that these activities occurred on both coasts over a span of 36 years. He gave us a detailed tour of his on-site production facility and we learned much about what it takes to make premium sparkling wines, too much to incorporate into this story. Therefore, be sure to read Barry's in-depth interview at **www.WineWherever.com**.

Equinox owner and winemaker Barry Jackson

Paul Masson introduced sparkling wines in this region in the 1880s and Martin Ray picked up the reins when he purchased Masson's winery in 1936 (see page 144). Ray continued making sparkling wines at Masson under his own label until his death in 1976. The Jacksons are now carrying on this legacy. "We are one of 16 dedicated Méthode Champenoise producers in California, out of 3,000 plus bonded wineries," Barry explained, noting that of those 16 producers, six are American-owned companies, of which they are one. "The other companies in California are located in the Carneros District of Napa and Sonoma and the Anderson Valley in Mendocino County."

The Jackson's two adult children are involved in the family business. Their oldest son Jeremy helps in the tasting room and their

younger daughter Ashley is working toward an enology degree at the
University of California at Davis and will "follow in her dad's footsteps," predicted Jennifer.

The hosts of hosts, the Jacksons offer several exclusive services to
their clients, including custom champagne bottling and wine-tasting
classes. Check their website to learn more. And while you're there, be
sure to click into a link labeled "Savory Selections"—here you'll find an
extremely detailed listing of champagne/wine and food pairings.

WINE MYTH "You can make money doing this." — *Barry Jackson*

Equinox is part of the Surf City Vintners' group. This winery
assemblage encompasses a two block radius, and Equinox is just a few
blocks away from the main cluster of wineries. Located in the same
building as Copious Winery (see page 188), Equinox's entrance is
around back where the parking lot dead ends. It's best to park in the
main lot and walk the very short distance to their tasting room. Once
inside, you'll find that the tasting area shares space with their champagne production facility, which is fascinating because you'll see different machinery than you'd see in an average winery. If it's not busy, and
Barry is there, ask for a quick tour. You won't be disappointed.

FEATURED WINE: Sparking Blanc de Blanc and Brut; Merlot and Rhone blends
TASTING COST: $5, waived with purchase
HOURS: Friday-Sunday, 12 PM-5 PM
LOCATION: 427-C Swift Street, Santa Cruz
PHONE: 831-423-3000
WEBSITE: www.equinoxwine.com
GPS COORDINATES: 36.956558, -122.04882

Santa Cruz

13 Hillcrest Terrace Winery

Joseph "Joe" Miller loves to make wines that pair well with food. This may seem an obvious rule-of-thumb for all winemakers, but for Joe, who co-owns Hillcrest Terrace Winery and is the winemaker there, it goes much further. "Wines enhance meals, and good food pairings enhance wines. This partnering of wine and food is well understood in many places of the world where wine has been a part of their culture for centuries, but it is not a part of U.S. tradition," Joe explained.

Winemaking started as a hobby for Joe more than 35 years ago. A longtime professor of astronomy and astrophysics at the University of California at Santa Cruz, Joe, who has since retired, also was for 14

Winery co-owner and winemaker Joe Miller

years the director of the Lick Observatory, located at the top of Mt. Hamilton in the Diablo Range. To add to his list of accomplishments, Joe spent 30 years teaching wine appreciation at the university and has traveled the world's major wine regions, including Australia, Italy and France. "My winemaking approach has been heavily influenced by French wines," Joe said. "Wine is seen as part of the overall culture of food and dining in France. French wines tend not to be overly alcoholic or overly extracted. They do not show strong flavors contributed by the wood of barrels, as many California wines do. They tend to have higher acidity levels than California wines. Their overall balance often leads to a better matching with food."

Hillcrest Terrace Winery, which opened in 2008, purchases all of its grapes from Santa Cruz Mountain vineyards, working with growers to secure fruit that will produce well-balanced wine without excessive alcohol. The winery offers a good selection of wines, and this is important, according to Joe. "Different people like different kinds of wine," he says. "Variety is important. What makes me feel best of all is when people say things like 'I really like this place' or 'I really like your wines.' Comments like that make you feel you are on the right track and that all those hours you worried over the wines were worth it."

Joe's business partner is Kurt Grutzmacher. It was Kurt who talked Joe into making his hobby a full-time gig, but Joe gives grand nods to Kurt. "The winery wouldn't exist without him," Joe said. "He tasted the homemade wines I made for years and said they were better than most things he could buy. He said we should start a winery. I said no way." But eventually Kurt got his way and the two haven't slowed down since. Joe is responsible for all the winemaking duties with the help of associate winemaker and son Sam Miller, and Kurt takes care of all the financial and managerial aspects of the business, including operating the tasting room and outside sales.

> **WINE MYTH** "Sulfites in wines cause allergic reactions." — *Joe Miller*

Hillcrest Terrace Winery is part of the Surf City Vintners group, but it is across the street from the main concentration of wineries. They have great signage so you should have no problem finding it. The tasting room, which shares space with their winery and barrel room, is stylishly fun and refreshing. When we visited, the bar was full of wine lovers enjoying themselves.

Having taught for 30 years, Joe is planning on offering wine appreciation classes at his winery. "The old professor in me can't resist explaining a few things when people clearly want to understand more about wine, but I think I do it in an easy-going, relaxed way," Joe shared. "I simply can't educate every person that a wine of ours that isn't to their liking at first may be to their liking if they understood it better." He also shared that visitors really enjoy meeting him and getting a chance to chat with a winemaker. "As a scientist and professor, I spent a lot of time alone in my office thinking about the universe or discussing it with a few colleagues or advanced students. I also lectured to large classes. But none of that is like standing at the tasting bar and greeting everyone who walks through the door." To learn more about Joe, read his winemaker interview at **www.WineWherever.com**.

FEATURED WINE: Pinot Noir, Chardonnay and Merlot
TASTING COST: $5
HOURS: Saturday and Sunday, 12 PM-5 PM
LOCATION: 429-B Ingalls Street, Santa Cruz
PHONE: 408-426-1500
WEBSITE: www.hillcrestterracewinery.com
GPS COORDINATES: 36.958466, -122.048243

14 MJA Vineyards

M JA Vineyards is one of Santa Cruz's newest wineries. Owner Marin John Artukovich—whose initials make up his winery's name—arrived in Santa Cruz by way of Napa, where he had a winery already. But before that, he was in Hawaii, where he was a coffee king.

Originally from Southern California, in the early 1990s Marin left California for the big island of Hawaii and its Kona Coast, taking with him his new wife and baby son John. The couple purchased a Kona coffee bean plantation and launched KOA Coffee in 1995, a green coffee broker and supplier to large businesses. In 2001, *Forbes* magazine named KOA Coffee the number one coffee in America. Because of this accolade, Marin launched a very successful online coffee business, roasting and selling Kona coffee directly to consumers.

In 2005, Marin and his wife divorced and the coffee business was sold in 2007. Marin found himself back in California, where he purchased an existing winery in St. Helena, Napa Valley. The 18-acre estate, of which 12 acres were already planted with Cabernet Sauvi-

gnon, was Judd's Hill Winery; Marin renamed his newest venture MJA Vineyards. After a major renovation, which included digging a 5,500-square-foot underground cave for wine storage, Marin opened his new winery to the public, but by appointment only.

As much as he liked the Napa Valley, Marin missed the beach, missed riding his beach cruiser bike and missed playing his favorite sport—beach volleyball. Now grown, Marin's son John was a student at Cabrillo College in Aptos, so his trips to the area were frequent. In 2010, Marin decided to transition his winery and his life to Santa Cruz and brought MJA Vineyards with him.

For now, Marin will continue to make wine using grapes from Napa and the Santa Cruz Mountains. But soon he will begin to use estate-grown grapes from the Santa Cruz Mountains. As part of the transition, Marin purchased 20 acres of prime land on Highland Road, where he is establishing a Pinot Noir vineyard. Rob Lloyd, Marin's winemaker from his Napa winery, will oversee winemaking duties in Santa Cruz, along with Mikael Wargin. Prior to joining MJA, Mikael was assistant winemaker and cellar rat at Burrell School Vineyards & Winery (see page 177) and winemaker at Vino Tabi (Santa Cruz).

Another great member of Marin's team is Cathy Bentley, who manages MJA's tasting room and public relations/marketing division. A former coffee shop roaster for many years in Capitola, Cathy became interested in the wine industry and desired a career change. She worked at Silver Mountain Winery's tasting room in Surf City for a while (see page 202) then joined Marin when he opened his Santa Cruz winery.

Cathy warmly greeted us when we arrived and gave us the quick tour of the Santa Cruz/Hawaiian-influenced tasting room, showing us photos of Marin's path from Kona to the Napa Valley to Santa Cruz. But what we noticed were the coffee beans for sale—Marin roasts them himself. Cathy then told us that Marin's coffee has won the very prestigious Gevalia Kona Coffee Cupping Competition. What is "cupping?" Cathy explained, "Cupping is when you put coffee grounds into a coffee cup, fill it with hot water and let it sit. Then you take a teaspoon and place it level in the cup so that the coffee fills the spoon and the grounds stay at the bottom. It's a way of tasting coffee. In a sense, cupping for coffee is like wine tasting for wine."

MJA is part of Surf City Vintners; their elegant tasting room is located in the complex near the New Leaf Market. They have fun special events, the most popular called "Wine Cellar Cinema." Movies are projected onto a large warehouse wall inside their winery. "People bring beach chairs and blankets and we have dinner, do some wine tasting and watch the movie. It's fun," Cathy said, noting that they have a movie trivia contest with great prizes. The cost is $20 per person and free for wine club members.

The winery has a second tasting room in the Santa Cruz Mountains near MJA's vineyards. Located in a beautiful mountain setting and surrounded by picnic tables in the redwoods, the tasting room looks like a small country lodge, with a wonderfully well-worn wooden interior and inviting indoor stone fireplace. They have great outdoor parties in the summer. It's worth the stop if you're in the area.

FEATURED WINE: Cabernet Sauvignon
TASTING COST: $5-$8

SANTA CRUZ TASTING ROOM
HOURS: Daily, 12 PM-6 PM
LOCATION: 328-A Ingalls Street, Santa Cruz
PHONE: 831-421-9380
WEBSITE: www.mjavineyards.com
GPS COORDINATES: 36.958945, -122.046529

SECOND TASTING ROOM: SANTA CRUZ MOUNTAINS
HOURS: Thursday-Sunday, 12 PM-5 PM
LOCATION: 24900 Highland Way, Los Gatos
PHONE: 408-353-6000
WEBSITE: www.mjavineyards.com
GPS COORDINATES: 37.1107, -121.911829

Santa Cruz

15 Santa Cruz Mountain Vineyard

Jeff Emery is more than the winery owner and winemaker at Santa Cruz Mountain Vineyard. He is also the truck driver, barrel washer, floor sweeper, grease monkey, fork lift operator and electrician. These are just a few of Jeff's self-admitted duties that, at many times, could apply to any small winery operation. Jeff specified that he felt "the public image of winemaking is all clean, fun and romantic. Folks don't know how many nerve-racking long days and late nights we go through when things don't work like they should. Ah, yes, the romance of winemaking!"

Jeff stumbled upon this romance when he was just a teenager. In 1979, he volunteered on a wine bottling line and that same year, was hired as a part-time cellar rat at Santa Cruz Mountain Vineyard. His boss was the winery's founder Ken Burnap. His fledgling winery was only four years old at the time, and having an extra set of hands

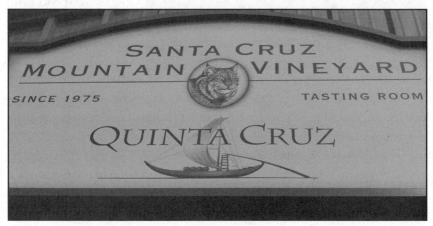

was helpful. Over the next two decades, Jeff worked with Ken—a winemaking legend—first as an apprentice, and then as a collaborator. When Ken retired in 2002, Jeff was overseeing the entire operation, including the winemaking. Finally, in 2004, Ken sold his vineyards on Jarvis Road to another party, but sold his winery to Jeff. Having to move the winery because of the sale of the vineyards, Jeff relocated first to Boulder Creek then to his present location in Santa Cruz.

Winery owner and winemaker Jeff Emery

A self-taught winemaker, Jeff has experienced more than 30 harvests thus far. When we inquired about his official winemaking schooling, Jeff laughed and told us a story about Ken: "When asked about whether he had looked for an officially-trained winemaker, Ken often was heard to say, 'I didn't want someone with a winemaking degree because I didn't want to have to spend time untraining them in order to make wine the way I wanted to make wine.'" The idea behind this approach is, according to Jeff, a bit more European and hands-off than the way a classic enologist would make wine. "One big example is the use of native yeast in our fermentations of Pinot Noir over the decades. UC Davis would say, 'Never use native yeast—it's too big of a risk.' We have used native yeast on the Estate Pinot from 1975 through 2003 and I continue to do so in many cases," Jeff said. It should be mentioned that Santa Cruz Mountain Vineyard is known for making a Pinot Noir that ages well for three decades.

In 2008, Jeff launched a second Santa Cruz Mountain Vineyard brand—Quinta Cruz. This label features only varietals that herald from the Iberian Peninsula, which encompasses the extreme southwest region of Europe. These Portuguese and Spanish varietals, which are slowly gaining favor with winemakers and wine lovers, include Tempranillo, Touriga Nacional, Touriga Franca, Souzao, Graciano and Tinto Cão. "What makes the Quinta Cruz brand rare and unusual is that it is the first brand in the United States dedicated only to varieties originally from the Iberian Peninsula," Jeff said. "There are many wineries who offer an Iberian variety or two, but none that I know of yet that have a brand only for California-grown Iberian varieties."

> **WINE MYTH** "That 'legs' on a glass mean anything about the wine."
> — *Jeff Emery*

If all this wasn't enough, Jeff—who has never held what he calls a "real job" in his life, never written a resume, filled out a job application or worn a tie—is a partner in a Soquel-based brandy company by the name of Osocalis. His role in the partnership is that of winemaker, creating the base wines from which the Cognac-style brandies are distilled. "I got involved with Osocalis because I think it is healthy to give yourself new challenges every decade or so to avoid complacency and boredom in your craft. Pulling the rug out from under yourself and learning new things is important in staying creative and innovative in something like winemaking." To learn more about Jeff, read his interview at **www.WineWherever.com**.

Santa Cruz Mountain Vineyard is part of the Surf City Vintners group. Here you can taste their wines in their tasting room, including the Quinta Cruz label, but unfortunately not the Osocalis brandy because of liquor laws. But they do have the brandy for sale, along with all of their wine offerings.

FEATURED WINE: Pinot Noir, Tempranillo, Grenache and Graciano
TASTING COST: $3
HOURS: Wednesday-Friday, 12 PM-5 PM; Saturday and Sunday, 12 PM-6 PM
LOCATION: 334-A Ingalls Street, Santa Cruz
PHONE: 831-426-6209
WEBSITE: www.santacruzmountainvineyard.com
GPS COORDINATES: 36.958697, -122.047935

Santa Cruz

16 Silver Mountain Winery

Silver Mountain Vineyards is home to 12 acres of Chardonnay, Pinot Noir and Merlot. But there's one very interesting fact about this straightforward statement, in that this special vineyard was the very first certified organic vineyard in the Santa Cruz Mountains.

Founder, owner and winemaker Jerold O'Brien never initially realized he was farming organically. "I work in harmony with Mother Nature, always have," Jerold said, plain and simple. He planted his vineyard in 1980, and it wasn't until the early 1990s that someone explained to him that his farming practices were considered organic. "I had never heard of the term 'organic,'" Jerold pointed out. Excited over this prospect, he contacted the California Certified Organic Farmers (CCOF) and they inspected his vineyards. "Normally, when one applies for organic certification, it's a three-year transition period. CCOF acknowledged I had been farming organically for ten years and certified me right away," Jerold said, with a grin.

As the leader of organic and sustainable practices in the region, Jerold continues

Jerold O'Brien and his wine dog Spencer

to make strides each and every day to work in unison with the environment. His list of accomplishments from his more than 30 years of sustainable and organic practices is too long and detailed to fit in this story, so we encourage you to read Jerold's interview at **www.Wine Wherever.com**, where you'll learn more about his passion for wine, flying (Air Force combat pilot and commercial pilot) and fishing!

Silver Mountain Winery opened in 1979, but was destroyed in the 1989 Loma Prieta earthquake. Before the quake, the winery simply was a small structure on a cement foundation. The aftermath of the quake gave Jerold the chance to completely design every aspect of his new winery. One major addition is what he calls his "Triple Green Canopy." We stood on a deck outside the tasting room with Jerold as he pointed to a nearby 6,000-square-foot steel roof, which towered over the press pad and winery below. With great pride, he explained the three "green benefits" of the mammoth structure: "First, it shades everything, greatly reducing the requirement for refrigeration and electricity," Jerold said. Pointing to the solar panels that covered the structure, he continued. "Second, this is the largest photovoltaic system in all of the Santa Cruz Mountains. It has

Silver Mountain's Triple Green Canopy

264 panels that generate 46 kilowatts at peak power and takes care of almost all of our electrical needs." He spoke more excitedly as he detailed the third benefit, "The 6,000 square feet of clean steel collects a lot of rainwater. In an average season, we'll get 35 inches of rain, about 120,000 gallons of rainwater. We use the water to irrigate the vineyards, as well as use it for processing in the winery. It is, in effect, a cistern system," Jerold concluded, noting that he plans on building additional storage to catch even more rainwater.

Inside the winery's tasting room, Jerold spoke of his winery's focus on three specific wines: Chardonnay, Pinot Noir and a blend called "Alloy." He explained that the Chardonnay is 100-percent organic grapes from his vineyard, which sits at an elevation of 2,100 feet. Next was the Pinot: "Pinot Noir is our second focus wine. We actually use Pinot from four different vineyards—three in the Santa Cruz Mountains and one in the Santa Lucia Highlands in Monterey County," Jerold said, noting that each are vineyard designated on the wine label, with no blending of grapes from the four vineyards. The third focus is their Bordeaux blend—"Alloy"—which is made from Cabernet Sauvignon, Merlot, Cabernet Franc and Petit Verdot. "In addition to the focus wines, we make a little bit of Rosé, Syrah and Cabernet Sauvignon. I say a little bit, but maybe 100 cases," Jerold said, smiling.

WINE MYTH "Sulfur in wine causes headaches." *— Jerold O'Brien*

You're probably wondering how Silver Mountain got its name, and there are two stories. The first one is that Jerold, a commodities future trader back in the 1970s, used profits from a silver trade to make the down payment on the property. The second is that on a foggy or rainy day, the rays of the setting sun cast a silvery shadow on the mountains behind the winery. You'll have to ask Jerold which story is correct!

Silver Mountain offers a second tasting room in west Santa Cruz. A part of the Surf City Vintners' group, this tasting room is open four days a week.

FEATURED WINE: Chardonnay, Pinot Noir, Syrah and a Bordeaux blend
TASTING COST: $5, waived with purchase

WINERY TASTING ROOM
HOURS: Saturday, 12 PM-5 PM
LOCATION: One Silver Mountain Drive, Santa
Cruz Mountains
PHONE: 408-353-2278
WEBSITE: www.silvermtn.com
GPS COORDINATES: 37.108539, -121.935609

TASTING ROOM: SURF CITY VINTNERS
HOURS: Thursday-Sunday, 12 PM-5 PM
LOCATION: 402 Ingalls Street #29, Santa Cruz
PHONE: 831-466-0559
WEBSITE: www.silvermtn.com
GPS COORDINATES: 36.958697, -122.047935

Santa Cruz

17 Sones Cellars

Michael Sones and Lois Dell met while both worked on an Italian cruise ship in 1987. Little did they know that many years later they would become winemakers and dual owners of their own winery.

Michael, a native of England, was a professional photographer. He worked many photography jobs, beginning in London and ending up on cruise ships that sailed the world. During one of those sailings, the ship docked in Alameda and Michael made a beeline to "the land of John Steinbeck." As a boy, he had read many of the great writer's novels, so a trip to the Monterey and Salinas area was a thrill. But duty called and Michael soon was back at sea and experiencing the rest

of the world, namely, the food and wine.

Lois entered the cruise ship world by way of her medical social work. With her master's degree in social work, she spent many years at Children's Hospital at Stanford helping children who had cancer, hemophilia and AIDS. Needing some time off, she took a massage therapist job on the *Carla Costa*, the same ship where Michael was working, which is where they met. Eventually Lois returned to solid ground and her home in Santa Cruz, with Michael visiting when he could. They married in 1993.

Michael received his degree in fermentation science, a precursor of the enology and viticulture degree, from the University of California at Davis in 1995. Even though Michael has the formal degree, Lois received the added bonus of learning right alongside Michael, both while he attended the university and in the winery. "We have a common goal, to make what we feel is 'California-style' wine, and fortunately, our taste in wine style is generally congruent," Lois revealed. "We agreed at the beginning of this journey that we wouldn't release any wine unless we both liked it. If either one of us doesn't like it, we keep working on it until we're both happy with it. It can make the process a bit long at times, but we're always both happy in the end."

Sones Cellars opened their doors in 2003 and their tasting room in 2008. They do not grow their own grapes, but purchase what they need from local vineyards. Zinfandel and Petite Sirah are the winery's main offerings, and the latter, the Sones feel, is underappreciated by the general public. "We find that many people think of Petite Sirah as a tannic monster, incapable of fruitiness or finesse. We know that if its naturally strong tannins are carefully managed, it can make a beautiful, full, deep and complex wine," Lois explained, noting they spend a lot of time in the tasting room educating visitors about the varietal. "We see that Petite Sirah is growing in popularity now, both with winemakers and wine drinkers, but many wine drinkers don't seem to have discovered it yet and we're here to remedy

that situation!"

As a remembrance of their meeting and falling in love on the high seas, Lois and Michael use a ship's figurehead as their winery's logo. This figurehead is that of a goddess and represents both England and California. On the great seal of California, Roman goddess Minerva is the focal point. "Minerva is the goddess from which the Romans developed Britannia, the symbol of Britain," Lois explained, referring to when the Roman Empire in AD 43 invaded that part of the British Isles, which is today's Scotland. The Romans gave the land the name "Britannia," using a female goddess for identification.

WINE MYTH "Petite Sirah is just a small Syrah grape." — *Lois Sones*

Sones Cellars' small tasting room, part of the Surf City Vintners' group, is darling. Sharing warehouse space with the winery, the tasting area is refreshing and lively, especially when the huge garage doors are open and more people can join the party! But for you non-party-goers, also known as designated drivers, Sones has a treat just for you! The gifts vary, but many times drivers will receive a decoratively wrapped chocolate truffle. And if you happen to see a young lady working the register when you visit, that's more than likely Michaela Sones, Lois and Michael's preteen daughter. Even though her favorite thing to do is to stomp grapes during the winery's annual fall grape-stomp event, Michaela also loves to dance around the winery and entertain visitors.

FEATURED WINE: Petite Sirah, Zinfandel and blends
TASTING COST: $3
HOURS: Friday-Sunday, 12 PM-5 PM
LOCATION: 334-B Ingalls Street, Santa Cruz
PHONE: 831-420-1552
WEBSITE: www.sonecellars.com
GPS COORDINATES: 36.958697, -122.047935

Santa Cruz

18 Vine Hill Winery

Vine Hill Winery is a great place to visit, if not for the amazing wine or spectacular view from their observation deck, then for its history. The site has hosted an operating winery and vineyard for more than 130 years.

Founded in 1877 as Jarvis Union Vineyard, original owner John W. Jarvis was an established leader in the Santa Cruz wine industry. Fourteen years earlier, he and his brother George purchased the 300-acre Rancho San Andreas and coined the area "The Vine Hill District." John went on to become the president of the Santa Cruz Mountain Wine Company, a business that produced approximately 80 percent of the nearly quarter of a million gallons of wine produced in 1890. He passed away two years later. Over the next 100 years, the land passed through many hands, including that of Ken Burnap, the founder of Santa Cruz Mountain Vineyard (see page 199). In 2004, a group of in-

It's a bit of a walk to the observation deck, but the view is worth the effort.

vestors purchased the winery portion of the property and aptly named it Vine Hill Winery.

One of those investing partners is Nick Guerrero, whom we met on the day of our visit. Always interested in wine, Nick received an undergraduate degree in fermentation science (the precursor to the enology and viticulture degree) from the University of California at Davis. Upon his graduation in 1987, Nick was a busy healthcare consultant, traveling all over the nation. The work began to drain him. "In reflecting on my family life and my quality of life, I thought of redirecting my energies from a life filled with extensive travel to a life

Vine Hill Winery's Nick Guerrero

with a more intrinsically rewarding lifestyle," Nick shared. "Owning and operating a winery has been a lifelong dream. I felt then, and still feel today, that I am a very lucky person for being able to successfully pursue my dream." We spent considerable time with Nick; you can read the entire interview at **www.WineWherever.com**.

Vine Hill Winery's winemaker is Sal Godinez. Sal spent the first ten years of his career at Freemark Abbey Winery (Napa Valley) then moved to Saintsbury Vineyards (Napa) in 1996. In 2005, he joined Vine Hill. "Sal is an artisan who creates his special wines in the vineyard, guides them through their development during fermentation and blends them into the final result during barrel aging," Nick said. "He focuses on making Pinot Noirs and Chardonnays that are consistently outstanding. His wines have garnered outstanding awards from magazines such as *Wine Enthusiast* and *Connoisseur's Guide* and competitions like the Orange County Fair and the California State Fair."

Today, Vine Hill's 13 acres of vineyards are planted with 6,000

Pinot Noir vines, 2,000 Chardonnay vines and 1,000 Syrah vines. Managing those vines is England-born Rachel Ormes. She originally moved to California to pursue the culinary arts, but decided after her arrival to focus on gardening and plants instead. Her horticulture studies took her to many California colleges and she ended up at the University of California in Santa Cruz, majoring in environmental studies. At Vine Hill, Rachel uses an organic approach to her farming.

> **WINE MYTH** "Mass produced wines can score higher than 90 in a blind tasting." — *Nick Guerrero*

It was Rachel who led us up the hill to the winery's observation deck. We soon learned that the deck was not an actual deck, but a grassy knoll with spectacular views of Monterey Bay. Inviting Adirondack chairs were perfectly placed so visitors can relax—with a glass of Vine Hill wine, of course—and absorb the view, the manicured gardens and, of course, "Rachel's" vineyard. When we asked about what this land means to her, Rachel, in her beautiful English accent, said many things. But the one thing that struck us most was her intense desire "to tap into the harmony of the farm."

We strongly recommend that you make the effort to visit the winery's tasting room when it is open the third weekend of every month. You can also visit Vine Hill's second tasting room in the Surf City Vintners' complex (opening late summer 2011).

FEATURED WINE: Pinot Noir, Chardonnay and Syrah
TASTING COST: $10 at winery; $5 at downtown Santa Cruz tasting room

WINERY TASTING ROOM
HOURS: Third weekend of the month, 12 PM-5 PM
LOCATION: 2300 Jarvis Road, Santa Cruz
PHONE: 831-427-0436
WEBSITE: www.vinehillwinery.com
GPS COORDINATES: 37.0728, -121.961806

TASTING ROOM: SURF CITY VINTNERS
HOURS: Thursday, 12 PM-5 PM; Friday and Saturday, 12 PM-8 PM; Sunday and Monday, 12 PM-5 PM
LOCATION: 402 Ingalls Street #21, Santa Cruz
PHONE: 831-427-0436
WEBSITE: www.vinehillwinery.com
GPS COORDINATES: 36.958697, -122.047935

19 Bargetto Winery

At 77 years and counting, Bargetto Winery is the oldest family-owned and -operated winery in the Santa Cruz Mountains. The winery and adjacent tasting room are based in Soquel, with another wonderful tasting room found on Monterey's famed Cannery Row (see page 47).

Heritage is the reason for the Bargetto family's longevity and success. Brothers Phillip and John Bargetto emigrated from northern Italy around the turn of the 20th century, bringing their winemaking experience with them. They settled in San Francisco and in 1910 opened South Montebello Vineyard and Wine Company. In 1918, the brothers moved south to Soquel, opening their new winery—Bargetto Winery—on the banks of Soquel Creek. They made and sold their Italian-styled wine from an old barn on the property during that first year, until Prohibition shut them, and most of the nation's alcohol-

based businesses, down in 1919. Not wanting to give up their business, they sold produce to local customers, but still made wine for friends and family on the side.

Prohibition was repealed in 1933. Because they had a winemaking enterprise already in place, the Bargetto brothers immediately launched a wine wholesale business and ran it in tandem with their popular wholesale produce enterprise. But six years later, tragedy hit when Phillip passed away, leaving John alone to run the family business, which he did into the 1950s. Eventually, John's sons Ralph and Lawrence officially joined in, helping their father carry on the Bargetto heritage of creating fine wines. The '60s and '70s were times of growth and innovation, as new state-of-the-art winemaking equipment was introduced and new varietals were added. Today, the third generation of Bargettos—Lawrence's kids Martin, John and Loretta—oversee the family business. And according to the younger John Bargetto, it's a challenge sometimes working with family. "Each has a strong Italian opinion," he said, but noted that it's equally good because the entire family is committed to carrying on their family legacy.

WINE MYTH "That legs of wine on a wine glass come from glycerol (actually alcohol)." — *John Bargetto*

Another key to Bargetto Winery's longevity has been their unwavering commitment to winegrowing sustainability. They adhere to three key tenets: to be environmentally sound (produce wines in a green manner); to be economically feasible (consistently produce quality wines that retain devoted customers and efficient business practices); and to be socially equitable (provide a healthy and dignified work environment for employees and give back to their community).

One way that Bargetto gives back is through the LA VITA Fund. "La Vita" means "the life" in Italian, and the LA VITA label is a unique blend of Dolcetto, Nebbiolo and Refosco, all Santa Cruz Mountains northern Italian red varietals from Bargetto's famed Regan Vineyard. With each release under the LA VITA name, a work of art is used for the label. These masterpieces depict the artists' portrayal of wine in art, from an 1881 Pierre-Auguste Renoir oil painting titled *Luncheon of the Boating Party*, selected for their 1998 release, to an 1875 oil painting by William-Adolphe Bouguereau titled *Vendangeuse (The Grape Picker)* for their 2002 release. Each year, a release party is held to unveil the new label, with proceeds going from the sale of the wine to a selected non-profit based in Santa Cruz County.

Another primary label at Bargettos is their "Chaucer's Cellars" dessert wine. These award-winning wines are produced from 100-percent pure fruit or natural honey. The label artwork is reminiscent of Medieval England, in the spirit of Geoffrey Chaucer's 14th century literary celebration, *The Canterbury Tales*.

When you visit Bargetto Winery, be sure to step out onto the back deck for a view of Soquel Creek. Throughout the year, the winery features musical events and art shows, so check their website for dates and times. The tasting room is open daily, with tours of the historic winery and cellar available by appointment.

FEATURED WINE: Chardonnay, Pinot Grigio, Pinot Noir and Merlot
TASTING COST: $5 for five tastes
HOURS: Daily, 11 AM-7 PM
LOCATION: 3535 North Main Street, Soquel
PHONE: 831-475-2258
WEBSITE: www.bargetto.com
GPS COORDINATES: 36.994721, -121.954406

20 Hunter Hill Vineyard and Winery

H unter Hill Vineyard and Winery, located a few miles northeast of
the Soquel, is both a wine lover's *and* hunter's paradise! Seriously!
There's no other way to describe it. If you like both, then you will be in
heaven when you visit.

When we arrived, owner Christine Slatter greeted us. Though
this was a surprise visit, Christine gave us a quick tour, which included
the meticulously manicured grounds, numerous seating areas, a waterfall and stream that leisurely drain into a large centerpiece pond and
rolling hills covered in vines. But what caught our attention was the
huge firepit and spit outside and the buffalo head mounted in the tast-

ing room. We just had to ask. "Vann shot the buffalo at Ted Turner's Vermejo Park Ranch in New Mexico," Christine clarified, referring to her husband Vann, an owner and winemaker at Hunter Hill.

All the members of the Slatter family are hunters and fishermen. "This really is who we are," Christine said. "I have hunted and fished with Vann and our sons throughout our lives." Inklings of this hunting family can be spied everywhere, from the well-used meat smoker outside to the moose antlers perched on top of the waterfall that cascades into the pond. And each May, the Slatters host a "Beast Feast" for their wine club members. The menu depends on the success of the hunt that year; past items have included elk carnitas, bison sliders and wild boar.

The Slatters became winery owners rather serendipitously. Christine's grandparents—Secondo and Sarafina Manildi—bought the land the Slatters now live and work on in 1904. Secondo was from Italy, and Sarafina, from Nevada. One of the first farms in the area, the Manildis raised apples, stone fruits and grapes from which Secondo made wine, giving bottles as gifts. The couple also reared their six children here.

In 1968, Christine and Vann and their two toddler sons moved  into her grandparents' home, which, at the time, was empty because her grandmother, then a widow, had gone to live with Christine's parents ten years earlier. "Vann had returned from three tours in Vietnam and we were just going to stay until we got on our feet," Christine said. But the couple loved the house and land so much they stayed. It wasn't until 1992 that the Slatters decided to replace the aging apple orchard with Merlot grapes. Then a friend suggested Vann try making wine, which he did. It was so good that the following year Vann made two varietals—Merlot and Pinot Noir—in the basement of the family home. The wines were a hit, so much so that Hunter Hill Vineyard and Winery opened their tasting room to the public in 1998.

Today, their property is planted in Merlot, Pinot Noir and Syrah, and a neighboring property is planted in Zinfandel. They release about 1,500 cases a year. Vann, who Christine describes as going "from a Navy Seal to a carpenter to a commercial fisherman to a general contractor to a winegrower," is a completely self-taught winemaker. Subscribing to a guiding principle that great wines are easy to make with well-loved, beautiful fruit, Vann certainly knows what he is doing. In 2005, his 2002 Syrah won a double-gold medal (98 out of 100 points) for Best of Show at the California State Fair!

Hunter Hill Vineyard and Winery came by the name in two ways. Indeed they are hunters who live on a hill, but mainly the Slatters named it for their late Chesapeake Bay Retriever. The family dog—a female by the name of Hunter—also was their duck-hunting partner. Hunter, who passed away in 1999, is memorialized on many of the winery's labels.

Another interesting hunting-themed label is their "Double Barrel" blend. On the label are two wine barrels and an old shotgun. "Since we had a blend of two French Rhone varietals, I thought it should be a really romantic kind of label," Christine disclosed, but Vann had other plans for the artwork. With two wines, he wanted to call it "Double Barrel." The old gun in the photo is one of Vann's favorite hunting antiques.

Hunter Hill's tasting room is located two miles from downtown Soquel. Their place overlooks The Forest of Nisene Marks State Park, a favorite hiking and mountain-biking destination in the area (see page 229).

FEATURED WINE: Pinot Noir, Syrah, Merlot and Zinfandel
TASTING COST: $5
HOURS: Saturday and Sunday, 11 AM-4 PM
LOCATION: 7099 Glen Haven Road, Soquel
PHONE: 831-465-9294
WEBSITE: www.hunterhillwines.com
GPS COORDINATES: 37.021691, -121.933039

Soquel 🍾🍾🍾🍾🍾🍾🍾🍾🍾🍾

21 Soquel Vineyards

Soquel Vineyards, owned by business partners Peter and Paul Bargetto and Jon Morgan, is named for the town it calls home. But another name you might recognize belongs to the two brothers, who are twins: they are part of the Bargetto winemaking legacy (see page 211). Peter and Paul are the grandsons of John Bargetto, who came to America from Italy in 1910 with his brother Phillip. In 1918, the brothers opened a winery in Soquel, just a year before Prohibition shut them down. When Prohibition was lifted in 1933, the brothers resumed their commercial winery business.

The three partners opened their winery and tasting room in 1987. They grow Pinot Noir grapes on the estate and purchase additional grapes from other vineyards as needed. "We do produce some Italian varieties: Sangiovese and Nebbiolo, grown at the Luna Matta Vineyard in Paso Robles," Peter revealed, when specifically asked about Italian varietals, considering their strong Italian heritage. Besides these

wines, the trio also concentrates on Cabernet Sauvignon, Chardonnay, Merlot, Pinot Noir and Zinfandel. Their annual release is around 4,500 cases.

Soquel Vineyards is alive with history, but you need to know where to look. For instance, the handmade Italian tiles on the roof of the tasting room date back to 1751. Peter tells customers that the roof is older than the Constitution! And the doors on the winery itself—which is located on the property—were made using a 12,000-gallon redwood tank from the old Bargetto family cellar. According to Peter, the wood itself is 1800-year-old first-growth redwood.

The winery and tasting room are located three miles out of Soquel. Open only on weekends, Soquel Vineyards rotates five different wines to taste on any given Saturday or Sunday. Just outside the tasting room is an inviting patio area—it is the perfect place to enjoy a glass of wine. The view is gorgeous, because just beyond the vineyard and rolling hills you can spot Monterey Bay. And be sure to watch for Peter's dog Midnight. A Golden Retriever, Midnight will happily accompany you on the patio!

FEATURED WINE: changes each weekend
TASTING COST: $5
HOURS: Saturday and Sunday, 11 AM-4 PM
LOCATION: 8063 Glen Haven Road, Soquel
PHONE: 831-462-9045
WEBSITE: www.soquelvineyards.com
GPS COORDINATES: 37.029858, -121.932562

Santa Cruz County

More Area Wineries

Boulder Creek
Ahlgren Vineyard
LOCATION: 20320 Highway 9, Boulder Creek
PHONE: 831-338-6071
WEBSITE: www.ahlgrenvineyard.com

Felton
Hallcrest Vineyards
LOCATION: 379 Felton Empire Road, Felton
PHONE: 831-335-4441
WEBSITE: www.hallcrestvineyards.com

Los Gatos
David Bruce Winery
LOCATION: 21439 Bear Creek Road, Los Gatos
PHONE: 408-354-4214
WEBSITE: www.davidbrucewinery.com

Santa Cruz
Bonny Doon Vineyards
LOCATION: 328 Ingalls Street, Santa Cruz
PHONE: 831-425-3625
WEBSITE: www.bonnydoonvineyard.com

Storrs Winery and Vineyards
LOCATION: 303 Potrero Street, Santa Cruz
PHONE: 831-458-5030
WEBSITE: www.storrswine.com

Vino Tabi
LOCATION: 334-C Ingalls Street, Santa Cruz
PHONE: 408-813-8384
WEBSITE: www.vino-tabi-wine.com

Saratoga
Big Basin Vineyards
LOCATION: 14598 Big Basin Way, Saratoga
PHONE: 408-564-7346

WEBSITE: www.bigbasinvineyards.com

Scotts Valley
Skov Winery
LOCATION: 2364 Bean Creek Road, Scotts Valley
PHONE: 831-438-4374
WEBSITE: www.skovwinery.com

Soquel
Poetic Cellars
LOCATION: 8000 North Rodeo Gulch Road, Soquel
PHONE: 831-462-3478
WEBSITE: www.poeticcellars.com

Winery Notes

Winery Notes

Winery Notes

Santa Cruz County

Side Trips

Big Basin Redwoods State Park

Big Basin Redwoods State Park is California's oldest state park. Located about 45 minutes from downtown Santa Cruz, it's a great place to enjoy a picnic and your Santa Cruz County wine, while being dwarfed by giant 2,000-year-old redwoods.

The park was created in 1902 and has grown from its initial 3,900 acres to more than 20,000 acres today. You can get trail maps and information about this gorgeous place in the main visitor center located near park headquarters. Across the road from the visitor center is an easy half-mile-long trail that meanders through some of the park's biggest and oldest trees. If you're into longer hikes, there's a 9.5 mile hike to beautiful Berry Falls. The trailhead also begins near park headquarters.

At the park, overnight accommodations are limited to campgrounds and a cluster of tent cabins. Reservations for both are generally required during summer (831-338-8860 or www.parks.ca.gov).

Santa Cruz Beach Boardwalk

Even though there is a fabulous beach in downtown Santa Cruz, it's the Santa Cruz Beach Boardwalk that attracts thousands of people each year. The destination has been around for more than a century and consistently is voted one of America's best seaside boardwalks.

Of its many attractions, the Boardwalk's Giant Dipper coaster is the most iconic. Since 1924, this huge wooden rollercoaster has thrilled more than 50 million people. It's one of those deceivingly tricky rides, slowly carrying you up to a spectacular view of Monterey Bay, then suddenly diving back to Earth, while you leave your stomach somewhere behind.

Another fun ride for both adults and kids is the Boardwalk's merry-go-round. The carousel is a 1911 classic created by Charles I. D. Looff. The German master carver immigrated to the U.S. in 1870 and six years later, carved the animals for Coney Island's very first merry-go-round. One fun fact is that the Santa Cruz carousel is one of the few remaining that still has its brass ring! You can test your aiming skill by grabbing the ring and throwing it into the clown's mouth (831-423-5590 or www.beachboardwalk.com).

After spending time at the Boardwalk, you may want to take a short drive to Surf City Vintners. Since it's a concentration of wineries within a two-block radius, you can walk and taste from one tasting room to the next (www.surfcityvintners.com).

Steamer Lane and the Santa Cruz Surfing Museum

If you want a bird's eye view of surfers riding Santa Cruz's famed waves, you have a chance to get it at what is known among locals as Steamer Lane. At this internationally-known surfing spot located at Lighthouse Point on West Cliff Drive, you can watch from the safety of a railed cliff as surfers negotiate the waves below.

Adjacent to the Steamer Lane viewing area is the Mark Abbott Memorial

Lighthouse, which doubles as the home of the Santa Cruz Surfing Museum. Here you'll learn about Santa Cruz surfing history, from the early days in 1886 when three Hawaiian princes surfed near the mouth of the San Lorenzo River, to the 1930s when young surfers rode their 60- to 90-pound homemade wooden boards, to now when technology has dramatically changed the sport of surfing (831-420-6289 or www. santacruzsurfingmuseum.org/museuminfo/index.html).

Natural Bridges State Beach

From the beginning of October through the end of February, tens of thousands of monarch butterflies winter at Natural Bridges State Beach in Santa Cruz. The parkland adjacent to the beach is filled with eucalyptus trees that provide the perfect shelter for the butterflies. Designated as the Monarch Grove, this natural preserve is the only one of its kind in the state. Entry is limited to an accessible boardwalk and observation area. Guided tours also are available.

These regal butterflies come here each year because of the abundance of their favorite food—milkweed. Since this is the only food that monarch caterpillars eat, you usually can find them or their bright green chrysalides (cocoons) attached to nearby fences or buildings.

This small 65-acre park is a fun place to visit any time of year. The beach—named for the natural sandstone arches that once stood in just offshore—offers a great view of the one remaining arch and of the waves crashing around its base. The sandy beach and tide pools are always great places to explore. And, if you're lucky, you might even spot a sea otter or whale (831-423-4609 or www.parks.ca.gov).

Santa Cruz Mission State Historic Park

Misión la Exaltacion de la Santa Cruz—now referred to as the Santa Cruz Mission State Historic Park and located in downtown Santa Cruz—was the twelfth mission in the series. Built in the early 1790s, like many of California's Jesuit missions, this one was severely damaged—not by earthquakes as one might guess, but by flood waters from the adjacent San Lorenzo River.

Yet the flooding was not to be this mission's primary nemesis. Just across the river from the mission, the Spanish founded a pueblo that became known as Villa de Branciforte. The new community built a racetrack and quickly became the local center for gambling, smuggling and other illegal activities. It drew workers and others away from the mission to where greater profits were possible. In 1818, Hippolyte de Bouchard, an Argentinean sea captain who became California's most infamous pirate, attacked and captured Monterey, flying the Argentine flag over the city for six days. Fear of attack quickly spread to nearby Santa Cruz, but it wasn't the pirate who attacked. Instead, men from Branciforte attacked and looted the mission. Over the years, the mission crumbled, and anything useful, from tiles to timbers, was taken by scavengers.

Today, a replica of the mission has been constructed near the original site. Surrounding the church is Santa Cruz Mission State Historic Park's complex of buildings, the oldest of which was built in 1791. The last of the mission's original buildings to survive, the single-story adobe has been restored to its original appearance (831-425-5849 or www.parks.ca.gov).

Wilder Ranch State Historic Park

Driving on Highway 1 just north of Santa Cruz, you will pass acre after acre of farmland. This area has been an agricultural treasure for more than two centuries. Tucked among the fields filled with Brussels sprouts, strawberries, pumpkins and dairy cows are old barns and farm houses, some abandoned, some still being used.

If you'd like to see how these farmers lived and worked, a visit to Wilder Ranch is highly recommended. This 7,000 acre coastal ranch is now a state historic park and features a working dairy, historic adobe buildings and an 1897 Victorian home. The cultural area of the park includes a rodeo arena, numerous ranch buildings and restored water-powered workshops.

After a day or two of wine and food pairings, you may be in the mood for a little exercise and Wilder Ranch is the perfect spot. Take your choice of trails—you can wander along the bluffs overlooking beaches or explore tide pools and sea caves. Better yet, take advantage of the 34 miles of multi-use trails for mountain biking, hiking or horseback riding that wind through redwood forests and open meadows (831-423-9703 or www.parks.ca.gov).

Año Nuevo State Reserve

Año Nuevo State Reserve, located on the coast near the town of Pescadero, definitely is not a petting zoo; it's nature in the raw. An outing can include witnessing a pregnant elephant seal cow give birth to a 75-pound pup or encountering a 15-foot-long, 5,000-pound bull elephant seal bellowing and snorting as he eyes you. Fortunately, the trained docents who lead the tours are good at keeping everyone at a safe distance.

The best time of year for watching elephant seals in action is usually the slowest time of year for the wineries—December through March. Winter marks the birthing and mating season, and hundreds of elephant seals will come ashore to engage in this annual ritual. You may see big bulls bellowing as they battle other males for control of harem females, younger bulls practicing false charges and other intimidations for future opportunities to mate with females or females trying to stay out of the way and keep their young pups safe.

If you time the weather right, a trip to witness the elephant seals, followed by wine tasting then cozying up in a B&B or hotel, is a wonderful winter getaway. If you don't mind the damp or the cold, traveling in the off-season can be more relaxing and inexpensive—fewer crowds, cheaper rates and more attention lavished from local businesses happy to see customers.

Año Nuevo State Reserve is open year-round and elephant seals generally are here all year. But during the birthing and mating season, access to the beach is by guided tour only. Elephant seal tour reservations during winter, and especially on winter weekends, are a must (650-879-0227 for recorded info, 800-444-4445 for winter reservations or www.parks.ca.gov).

The Forest of Nisene Marks State Park

The Forest of Nisene Marks State Park, located just north of Aptos, might not be a household name. But nearly every person in the U.S. knows of the 1989 Loma Prieta earthquake, and it is here where the epicenter of that destructive trembler can be found.

Nearly 100 years earlier—from the 1880s through the early 1920s—this land sat clear-cut of its old growth redwoods, which, back then, made many men rich, but scarred the mountains of this gorgeous area. Since then, the mountains have been healing themselves, regenerating second-growth redwoods, oaks and madrones that now cover much of the park's 10,000 acres.

Even though remnants remain of the old logging operation, including the mill site and a railroad trestle, the focused use of this land today is for recreation. The park's mountains rise from sea level to more than 2,600 feet and include 30 miles of trails for hiking and old dirt roads for mountain biking. Two of the park's most popular hiking destinations are to the quake's epicenter and Five Finger Falls. If you're looking for wildlife, expect to see the ubiquitous banana slugs, which seem to be found wherever there are redwoods. There are also numerous species of birds, and you might even spot a coyote or the more elusive bobcat or mountain lion.

The park is named for Nisene Marks whose family purchased the land from the lumber companies, hoping, but failing, to find oil beneath the denuded mountains. Nisene's children donated the property in her name, which also became the name of the state park (831-763-7062 or www.parks.ca.gov).

Corralitos Market and Sausage Company

Talk with anyone who lives in or near the small community of Corralitos and you'll soon learn that the Corralitos Market and Sausage Company is the place to go for the best sausage sandwiches to be found anywhere. Attesting to the market's popularity are its 3,000 Facebook friends—a large fan base for any small business—along with hundreds of comments by satisfied customers.

Located at 569 Corralitos Road, the small market sports a Mission-style front façade. Inside you can find just about anything you need for a picnic—wine, fresh produce, snacks and coffee. But it's the

meats, all fashioned on the premises, which are the market's claim to fame. You'll find a large selection of sausages smoked with local applewood; one favorite is the Cheesy Bavarian. Not into sausage? The market features about 60 other specialty meat products (831-722-2633; no website).

For More Information

Santa Cruz Mountains Winegrowers Association
7605-A Old Dominion Court
Aptos, CA 95003
831-688-6961
www.scmwa.com

Santa Cruz County Visitors Council
303 Water Street
Santa Cruz, CA 95060
800-833-3494
www.santacruzca.org

Stephanie Says!

Stephanie Anderson of Bray Vineyards (www.brayvineyards.com), located in California's Amador County, is one of our favorite tasting room managers. When it comes to wine tasting adventures and misadventures, Stephanie has seen it all.

For our *Wine Wherever* books and apps, we asked Stephanie to provide rules of etiquette for wine tasters. Thus the creation of "Stephanie Says!" Her tips are designed to inform and entertain, but mostly, so everyone—from wine lovers to tasting room staff—will have an enjoyable experience.

- Don't wear heavy perfume or cologne. They overwhelm a wine's subtle aromas and flavors, for you and for everyone around you.

- Never pick up a bottle and serve yourself! The winery could lose its license.

- Taste in the suggested order. Always taste from whites to reds to sweets. And remember, when you have sipped enough to taste, dump the rest. You don't have to drink all the wine you are poured.

- A tasting room is not a bar. Once served, step back and make room for others, especially if the tasting room is busy.

- Ask before you wander off through the vineyard. Remember, the winery is not a public park.

- Designate a driver—this will ensure a carefree day of tasting.

- Eat along the way—start with a good breakfast and snack throughout the day.

- Tasting room staff are often knowledgeable about local restaurants and places to stay. Some will even make reservations for you. Be sure to thank them with a wine purchase.

- Pack plenty of bottled water and drink it often—it mitigates the dehydrating effects of alcohol.

- Don't get wine-wasted. Only you will find yourself amusing.

- Avoid excess public displays of affection. Get a room!

- Call in advance if your group is larger than five so the winery can be ready. And be aware that some wineries have limited parking for buses and limousines or require reservations, so check before you go.

- Children are welcome at many wineries on non-event days; however, they need to be supervised! Tasting rooms are not play rooms! Whenever possible, leave the kids at home.

Stephanie at work behind the tasting bar.

- Don't roll into the tasting room five minutes before they close; that's not enough time to taste anything.

- And most importantly, if you like a wine you've tasted, buy a bottle or two!

From Dahlynn and Ken

Cheers!

We would be remiss if we did not acknowledge those people who helped us with the creation of this book.

First things first—family. To Dahlynn's teenage son Shawn: thanks for your patience while we researched, created and churned out yet another travel book. You're a great traveling partner and we appreciate your understanding, especially when we were nearing our deadline. And to Dahlynn's parents Cliff and Scharre Johnson: thanks for sending along all the newspaper and magazine clippings on the areas we were researching. It's such a treat to have our own personal clipping service!

Next, our publishing support crew: Roslyn Bullas for leading the charge; Terri Elders for her excellent editing and pointing out all of our dangling modifiers and verbal ticks; Bart Wright of Lohnes+Wright for creating all of our maps; Nancy Withers for being our "Girl Friday;" and Stephanie Anderson for her review of wine-tasting etiquette. Thanks!

We mustn't forget these important folks, all of whom helped in securing wineries in their respective areas: Rhonda Motil, executive director of the Monterey County Vintners and Growers Association (www.montereywines.org); Jane Howard, executive director of the Gilroy Visitor Bureau (www.gilroyvisitor.org); Karen Hibble, executive director of the Santa Cruz Mountains Winegrowers Association (www.scmwa.com); and Jules Robbins of Vines Online Solution (www.vinesos.com).

Two important people we must acknowledge lent their decades of combined enology and viticulture wisdom—Ridge Watson of Joullian Vineyards (Carmel Valley) and Paul Draper of Ridge Vineyards (Santa Cruz Mountains). Without your thoughtful guidance and unbridled patience when answering our technical questions, this book wouldn't have turned out so wonderfully well!

We must graciously thank our winery friends who offered their extra support, going above and beyond: Rhonda Boos, Angela Cesari, Herb Galindo, Jason Goelz, Emily Hirsch, Lore James, Mary Lindsay, Claire Marlin, Richard McCaw, Laura Ness, Anthony Pessagno and Christopher Watkins. And a special thank you to Jim O'Briant and his friend Kay Spencer; drinks are on us next time!

We owe our special travel partner Teresa Tjaden a big thank you. When Ken was unable to travel, Teresa filled in, accompanying Dahlynn to the Mid-Coast region. The gals have traveled many times before—from Southern California to Italy to Southeast Asia—and this trip turned out just as fun and memorable for these two best friends.

We mustn't forget the "home team"—our wonderful friends and neighbors who fed our pooches and picked up the mail while we were on research trips: Michele and Ken Cemo, Bill Falkenstein and Nikki and Jim Garner. Hope you all enjoyed the wine and goodies we brought home each time!

Last, a very sincere thank you to all the winery owners in this book for providing us with information and access to their properties for our research and photo shoots. And to those of you who sent bottles of their wines home with us, you are very much appreciated. Cheers!

INDEX

Up Close and Personal with Dahlynn and Ken McKowen

Ken and Dahlynn being silly in Ho Chi Minh Square, Hanoi, Vietnam.

Ken's favorite food is ice cream, Dahlynn collects Asian vases and they both are very fond of traveling, having trekked more than 200,000 miles in the last four years (if Dahlynn stays home too long, she gets antsy—blame it on her gypsy blood).

Ken (in the funny hat) is madly stomping grapes in a losing effort at a celebrity grape-stomping contest.

Dahlynn's favorite treat is tangerine-flavored Jelly Belly candy; Ken is a master woodworker and builds furniture, guitars and kayaks from scratch (no kits) and the couple's sole television is more than 30 years old. They don't have cable, but they do have one of those infamous converter boxes!

Ken loves to cycle (working off that ice cream), Dahlynn's favorite room is the kitchen where she creates gourmet meals using her huge collection of cookbooks (another reason Ken cycles) and the couple calls a small community near Sacramento, California, home.

Dahlynn enjoys spending time on their property (which features an 1880s Western theme town—really!), and Ken can often be found puttering in his large garden. Between them, they have three children, two grandchildren, one godson, two dogs and a parakeet named Fred.

Already having earned several college degrees, Ken remains the perpetual student and is nearly always the oldest in his college classes, Dahlynn crochets blankets and donates them to charitable organizations and the two spend countless hours volunteering in their local school district and for their local library.

Ken enjoys a glass of wine at the world's highest wine bar, the 360 Restuarant in Toronto's 1,815-foot tall CN Tower.

Because they are also business partners, Ken and Dahlynn are together 24/7, which, for some couples, could prove difficult. But not for these two; they wouldn't change a thing and absolutely love their lifestyle. Two days are never the same, which is fine with them. Needless to say, there is never a dull moment in the McKowen household!

Dahlynn and Ironstone Vineyards' executive chef James Lehman conducting a cooking demonstration at the winery.

Dahlynn and Ken relaxing at home in their backyard.

The Professional Side of Dahlynn and Ken McKowen

Together, Dahlynn and Ken McKowen have accumulated nearly 60 years of professional writing, editing, publication, marketing and public relations experience. Full-time authors and travel writers, when they passed a total of 2,000 articles, stories, books and photographs published, they stopped counting!

A writing highlight has been serving as coauthors and consultants for the famed *Chicken Soup for the Soul* series, where they collaborated with founders Jack Canfield and Mark Victor Hansen for more than a decade. Their titles completed with Jack and Mark include *Chicken Soup for the Entrepreneur's Soul*; *Chicken Soup for the Soul in Menopause*; *Chicken Soup for the Fisherman's Soul*; and

Good friend Teresa Tjaden assists Dahlynn as she signs copies of *Chicken Soup for the Entrepreneur's Soul* for more than 900 people at a Cookie Lee conference in Anaheim, California.

Chicken Soup for the Soul: Celebrating Brothers and Sisters. They have also edited and ghost-created many more books for this company.

Another facet of the couple's writing career is working one-on-one with the nation's top entrepreneurs and CEOs, providing ghost-writing and editing services. Their integrity and reputation is such that they have ghostwritten for a former President, more than two dozen Fortune 100 and 500 founders and a few California governors. And Dahlynn sits on the induction committee for the EPICENTER: International Entrepreneur Hall of Fame in Atlanta, Georgia, where she will help shape this organization and assist in fundraising for its new state-of-the-art building and entrepreneur-driven educational facility.

On the travel side, the McKowens have written the national award-winner *Best of California's Missions, Mansions and Museums*, as well as *Best of Oregon and Washington's Mansions, Museums and More* and *The Wine-Oh! Guide to California's Sierra Foothills,* all for acclaimed publisher Wilderness Press.

Under their own publishing house—Publishing Syndicate—the McKowens are creating several new books and anthology series with

noted authors. And wanting to continue the success of their wine books, the McKowens will release the *Wine Wherever* series under their own publishing house, with new books in production including one on the Paso Robles region of California. If that's

While Dahlynn signs books, Ken picks errant stems from de-stemmed grapes during a grape harvest.

not enough, they are also the creators of 13 iPhone winery-destination journaling apps under the *Wine Wherever* brand.

To learn more about the McKowens, please visit
www.PublishingSyndicate.com.

More Travel and Winery Books

by

Dahlynn and Ken McKowen

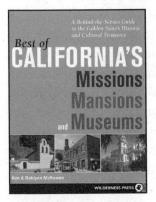

This national award-winning book features a behind-the-scenes look at 135 of California's historic and cultural treasures. From old Spanish missions to great art museums, there is something here for people of all ages. Features trivia questions, self-guided tours, contact information and websites. (368 pages)

ISBN 978-0-89997-348-2 Cover price $21.95

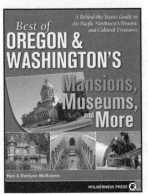

The McKowen's second book in their "Best of" travel series features 137 destinations in Oregon and Washington. They provide a behind-the-scenes look at historic forts, beautiful Victorian mansions and both small town and world-class museums. You will also find trivia questions, locator maps and contact information.(384 pages)

ISBN 978-0-89997-487-3 Cover price $21.95

The second in the popular *Wine Wherever* winery-destination series, this book features California's Paso Robles/Northern San Luis Obispo County wine region. More than 60 wineries are included, as well as maps, side trips, contact information and GPS coordinates for all of the wineries. (256 pages)
(Available August 2011)

ISBN 978-0-9824654-6-2 Cover price $15.95